Cook It Light
One-Dish
Meals

Also by Jeanne Jones

The Calculating Cook 1972

Diet for a Happy Heart 1975

Secrets of Salt-Free Cooking 1979

The Canyon Ranch Cookbook 1984

Cook It Light 1987

Eating Smart 1991

Jeanne Jones Entertains 1992

Cook It Light Classics 1992

Cook It Light Pasta, Rice, and Beans 1994

Light and Hearty 1994

Cook It Light Desserts 1994

Cook It Light One-Dish Meals

Jeanne Jones

Macmillan • USA

MACMILLAN
A Simon & Schuster Macmillan Company
1633 Broadway
New York, NY 10019-6785

Design by Levavi & Levavi

MACMILLAN is a registered trademark of Macmillan, Inc.
Library of Congress Cataloging-in-Publication Data
Jones, Jeanne.
Cook it light one-dish meals / Jeanne Jones
p.   cm.
Includes index.
ISBN: 0-02-860353-2 (alk. paper)
1. Entrees (Cookery) 2. Quick and easy cookery. I. Title.
TX740.J66 1996
641.8′2—dc20   95-35416   CIP
Manufactured in the United States of America
10 9 8 7 6 5 4 3 2 1

*This book is dedicated with both sincere thanks and
deep appreciation to the millions of people
who read my column, "Cook It Light," each week.
Your letters guide all of my work.*

Contents

Acknowledgments

In grateful acknowledgment: Tracy DeMas, recipe development and testing; William Hansen, organization of manuscript; Margret McBride, my agent; Jane Sigal, my editor.

Introduction

The end of every century is typically a time for looking back on things with nostalgia. Perhaps this explains the enormous number of requests I am getting from my readers to revise their mothers' and grandmothers' casserole dishes.

It wasn't too long ago that casseroles were retro, and one-dish meals in general were definitely *out*. I am delighted to have them back *in* again. In fact I'm so pleased about the whole idea of making meal preparation faster, easier, and less expensive that I am devoting this entire book to one-dish meals.

A one-dish meal differs from a regular entree in that it virtually makes a complete meal by itself. Also, a one-dish meal usually means there's only one serving dish. Often the pot or casserole used to prepare the dish doubles as the serving dish, making dinner portable and cleanup easy.

Although many casseroles are indeed one-dish meals, by no means are all one-dish meals casseroles. The one-dish meal category also includes soups, salads, pastas, soufflés, quiches, gratins, stews, roasts, pies, and even dishes *en papillote*. The usual meaning of *en papillote* is a single serving cooked in a paper or foil case, but I extend the definition to include a whole chicken!

Quite a few of the recipes in this book are revisions of recipes sent to me by my "Cook It Light" readers. But when revising their recipes to be lower in calories, fat, cholesterol, and sodium, it was not always possible to eliminate all the fat without losing the taste and texture of the original recipe. Simply, fat carries flavor and aroma. Fat also gives food texture, or mouth feel. For these reasons, while my versions are considerably lower in fat than the originals, some of them may still have over 30 percent of the calories coming from fat. In these cases, remember that the less than 30 percent fat recommended by the American Heart Association is for a whole day, not for each individual dish. By balancing higher fat dishes with low or nonfat dishes, you can still keep your calories in line and your daily allotment of fat grams at or below recommended levels.

When trying to make dishes as low in fat as possible, remember that it is aroma that creates flavor. The tongue tastes only sweet, salt, sour, and bitter. Every other flavor is created by the sense of smell, and it is often the fat that carries the aroma. You can't just take all the fat out and expect it to taste the same because it won't. It will taste flat and often lack balance.

To achieve more flavor in low-fat recipes, you need to get the maximum amount of aroma out of every ingredient you use. Add herbs and spices extravagantly, always crushing dried herbs using a mortar and pestle until you can smell them all over the kitchen. Choose a flavored oil or a naturally aromatic oil such as extra-virgin olive oil or dark sesame oil. Toast all nuts and seeds to enhance their flavor so that you need fewer of them. Use only the highest quality, most aromatic cheeses available such as Parmigiano Reggiano, Pecorino Romano, or a very sharp Cheddar. Whenever possible, sprinkle both nuts and cheese over the top of a dish to stimulate the senses of both sight and smell. When you do this, the perception is always that you have used more.

Balance can often be achieved by adding something acidic like vinegar or citrus juice or even buttermilk or yogurt to replace a dairy ingredient. Also helpful for brightening flavor through stimulation of the taste buds are all of the super-hot additives in the category I call "pleasing pain," such as Tabasco, chili oil, cayenne pepper, or red-pepper flakes.

Because cholesterol is found only in foods of animal origin, I routinely decrease the portion sizes of fish, poultry, meat, high-fat dairy products, and egg yolks and increase the amounts of vegetables, fruits, and grains. Since fiber is found only in foods of plant origin, specifically the complex carbohydrates, this ratio also automatically creates a lower cholesterol, higher fiber diet.

Due to the fact that many of these recipes contain canned, bottled, and boxed convenience foods, which greatly shorten the preparation time, they are also higher in sodium. Again, however, the 2,400-milligram recommendation for the amount of sodium you should not exceed per day is for just that—an entire day. Therefore, if one of your meals during any day is particularly high in sodium, combine it with other meals for that day that are not.

All recipes should be used as guidelines, not as hard-and-fast rules to be followed without deviation. Using your imagination, the ingredients you have on hand, and the recipes in this book, you can have lots of fun creating your own *Cook It Light One-Dish Meals.*

Jeanne Jones

Salads
and Stuffed
Vegetables

Greek Pasta Salad

⋺

This salad is a revision of a recipe sent to me by a reader in St. Paul, Minnesota. She asked me to lower the amount of oil in the dressing. The secret is to use the most flavorful oil you can find, reduce the amount called for, and make up the difference in volume with a nonfat alternative such as yogurt, fat-free mayonnaise, wine, stock, or water.

Salad

12 ounces rotelle pasta, cooked al dente, drained, and cooled
1/4 pound feta cheese, coarsely crumbled (3/4 cup)
1/4 pound lightly steamed fresh or thawed frozen snow peas (1 1/2 cups)
1/2 red bell pepper, cut into strips (2/3 cup)
1/2 green bell pepper, cut into strips (2/3 cup)
1 cup cherry tomatoes, halved
1/2 large red onion, finely diced (1 cup)
One 2 1/4-ounce can sliced black olives, drained

Dressing

1/2 cup nonfat plain yogurt
1/4 cup red wine vinegar
2 tablespoons extra-virgin olive oil

1 teaspoon dried oregano, crushed
1 tablespoon fresh mint, finely chopped
¼ teaspoon salt
¼ teaspoon freshly ground black pepper

1. In a large bowl, combine all the salad ingredients and mix well.

2. In a small jar or bowl, combine all the dressing ingredients and shake or mix well. Pour all but ¼ cup of the dressing over the salad and mix well. Chill, tightly covered, in the refrigerator.

3. Fifteen minutes before serving, remove the salad from the refrigerator and mix in the remaining dressing.

Makes 11 cups, or six scant 2-cup servings

Each serving contains approximately
Calories: 353
Fat: 11 g
Cholesterol: 17 mg
Sodium: 405 mg

Wild Rice and Baby White Lima Bean Salad à l'Orange

ᦓ

The slight chewiness of the wild rice combined with the smoothness of the baby limas and goat cheese and the crunchiness of the toasted almonds create a wonderful contrast in textures. The color and variety of ingredients in this salad give it enormous eye appeal and also offer a superb nutritional profile.

To intensify the flavor of this unusual and delicious vegetarian salad, I like to cook the wild rice in orange juice and sherry. For two cups of cooked wild rice, in a medium-size saucepan, combine ½ cup raw wild rice with 2 cups orange juice, 1 cup sherry, ½ teaspoon salt, 1 teaspoon dried thyme, and 1 tablespoon freshly grated orange zest. Bring it to a boil over high heat and then reduce the heat to low and cook it, covered, for 1 hour.

Dressing

¼ *cup sherry vinegar*
½ *teaspoon salt*

$^1\!/_2$ *teaspoon freshly ground black pepper*

$^1\!/_2$ *teaspoon dried thyme, crushed*

2 teaspoons sugar

1 tablespoon Dijon mustard

$^1\!/_2$ *cup orange juice*

1 tablespoon freshly grated orange zest

Salad

2 cups cooked wild rice

2 cups cooked baby white lima beans

4 cups assorted young salad greens, torn into bite-size pieces

2 cups diced peeled orange

2 ounces goat cheese, crumbled

*2 tablespoons chopped almonds, toasted in a 350°F oven until golden,
8 to 10 minutes*

1. In a small jar or bowl, combine all the dressing ingredients and shake or mix well.

2. Combine the wild rice and beans in a medium-size bowl. Add the dressing and mix well. Cover and allow to stand at room temperature for at least 30 minutes; all day is even better.

3. To serve, arrange 1 cup of the greens on each of four plates. Top the greens with 1 cup of the rice and bean mixture. Top each salad with $^1\!/_2$ cup of the orange and 2 tablespoons of the cheese. Sprinkle $^1\!/_2$ tablespoon of the almonds over each serving.

Makes 4 servings

Each serving contains approximately
Calories: 399
Fat: 10 g
Cholesterol: 12 mg
Sodium: 839 mg

Classy Clam Salad

ᔓ

This quick, easy, and unusual seafood salad is sure to be a hit with your family and friends. It is an ideal party dish for luncheons and light supper menus any time of the year. It is also a wonderful meal in minutes for just one or two people. For this reason, I have written the recipe for four servings, which can easily be divided or multiplied to fit your serving needs.

This salad is even faster and easier to make if you buy the prewashed, pretorn greens available in sealed packages in the produce sections of most supermarkets.

Sometimes, instead of sourdough, I like to serve this salad with whole-wheat toast triangles.

---

1 ½ tablespoons extra-virgin olive oil
2 cloves garlic, pressed or minced
¼ teaspoon freshly ground black pepper
1 ½ teaspoons Worcestershire sauce
2 tablespoons fresh lemon juice
Two 6 ½-ounce cans chopped clams, undrained
¼ cup freshly grated Parmesan or Romano cheese
8 cups assorted young salad greens, torn into bite-size pieces
4 plum tomatoes, diced
8 slices sourdough bread

1. Combine the olive oil and garlic in a small skillet or saucepan and cook over medium heat just until the garlic sizzles, about 1 minute. Remove the skillet from the heat and allow the mixture to cool for a few minutes. Add the pepper, Worcestershire sauce, and lemon juice, and mix well. Pour the mixture into a large bowl.

2. Drain the clams, reserving 2 tablespoons of the clam juice. Add the drained clams, the reserved juice, and the cheese to the ingredients in the bowl and mix well. Add the greens to the bowl and toss thoroughly.

3. To serve, arrange 2 cups of the salad on each of four plates and top each serving with one-quarter of the tomatoes. Serve the sourdough bread on the side.

Makes 4 servings

Each serving contains approximately
Calories: 265
Fat: 9 g
Cholesterol: 21 mg
Sodium: 507 mg

Grilled Chicken Salad

ᒍ

This recipe can easily be adapted for summer entertaining when you can use an outdoor barbecue. Grill
the chicken instead of broiling it and use fresh summer
corn in place of the canned corn.

---

4 boneless, skinless chicken breast halves, all visible fat removed
2 tablespoons extra-virgin olive oil
2 cloves garlic, pressed or minced
1 teaspoon chili powder
$1/2$ teaspoon salt
$1/4$ teaspoon freshly ground black pepper
1 teaspoon freshly grated lime or lemon zest
3 tablespoons fresh lime or lemon juice
Two 11-ounce cans salt-free whole-kernel corn, drained
One 16-ounce can black beans, rinsed and drained
2 plum tomatoes, cut into wedges
1 medium-size red onion, thinly sliced
$1/4$ cup chopped fresh cilantro, or to taste
Lime or lemon wedges, for garnish (optional)
Fresh cilantro sprigs, for garnish (optional)

1. Cook the chicken on a grill or under a broiler until it has lost its pink color and is completely opaque, about 4 minutes per side. Do not overcook or the chicken will be too dry. Cut the grilled chicken diagonally into ½-inch slices and set aside.

2. Heat the olive oil in a large, heavy skillet or saucepan over medium heat. Add the garlic and cook just until it sizzles, about 1 minute. Add the chili powder and cook, stirring constantly, for 30 more seconds. Remove the skillet from the heat, add the salt, pepper, lime or lemon zest, and juice, and mix well. Add the corn and beans and mix well.

3. Spoon the mixture into a large bowl. Add the chicken, tomatoes, onion, and cilantro and toss thoroughly. Serve immediately, garnished, if desired, with the lime or lemon wedges and the sprigs of cilantro.

Makes six 1 ½-cup servings

Each serving contains approximately
Calories: 305
Fat: 8 g
Cholesterol: 48 mg
Sodium: 523 mg

Warm Chicken Salad with Honey–Rosemary Vinaigrette

☞

For a variation on this recipe, try substituting maple syrup for the honey.

Vinaigrette
2 tablespoons herb vinegar
$1/4$ cup honey
$1/4$ teaspoon salt
$1/4$ teaspoon freshly ground black pepper
$1/4$ teaspoon dried rosemary, crushed
$1/4$ teaspoon finely grated lemon zest
1 tablespoon extra-virgin olive oil

Salad
$1/4$ cup chopped walnuts
4 boneless, skinless chicken breast halves, all visible fat removed
6 cups assorted young salad greens, torn into bite-size pieces
4 whole-grain rolls

1. Combine all the vinaigrette ingredients, except the olive oil, in a medium-size saucepan and bring to a boil over medium heat. Remove the saucepan from the heat and slowly add the oil, stirring constantly. Set aside.

2. Put the walnuts in a large, nonstick skillet and cook, stirring frequently, over medium heat until fragrant and toasted, about 5 minutes. Watch them carefully because they burn easily. Put the toasted walnuts in a bowl and set aside.

3. Lightly spray the chicken breast halves with nonstick vegetable spray and place them in the same skillet. Cook over medium-low heat until they have lost their pink color and are completely opaque, about 5 minutes per side. Do not overcook or they will become tough.

4. To serve, arrange 1 ½ cups of the greens on each of four plates. Thinly slice each chicken breast half and place it on top of the greens. Spoon ¼ cup of the vinaigrette over each serving. Top each salad with 1 tablespoon of the toasted walnuts. Serve with a whole-grain roll.

Makes 4 servings

Each serving contains approximately
Calories: 346
Fat: 11 g
Cholesterol: 67 mg
Sodium: 387 mg

Curried Rice and Smoked Chicken Salad

ꝏ

I spent one Christmas at Enchantment Resort, a beautiful hideaway nestled in the red rock cliffs of Sedona, Arizona. The Christmas Day buffet, created by their talented executive chef, Jerry Peters, was an amazing display of all the traditional holiday dishes. Among the less traditional selections, however, was a curried rice and smoked chicken salad that was so unusual and so delicious that I practically made it my entire holiday meal.

I later asked Jerry if he would give his recipe to me so that I could share it with my readers. I have made a few small changes in the original recipe to lower the percentage of fat in each serving, but the flavor remains the same. I am certain that you will share my enthusiasm for this fabulous salad.

If you are planning to make it ahead of time, wait until you are ready to serve it to add the toasted almonds so that they will be crunchy.

Salad

$^{1}/_{2}$ cup shelled almonds, chopped

1 pound smoked chicken meat, cut into $^{1}/_{2}$-inch dice

4 cups cooked rice

$^{1}/_{2}$ cup chopped green onions (scallions)

$^{1}/_{2}$ cup bias-sliced celery

$^{1}/_{4}$ cup diced red bell pepper

1 large mango (11 ounces), peeled and diced (about 1 cup)

One 8-ounce can sliced water chestnuts, drained (1 cup)

One 10 $^{1}/_{2}$-ounce can mandarin orange segments, packed in juice,
    drained (1 cup)

Dressing

$^{1}/_{2}$ cup fat-free mayonnaise

$^{1}/_{4}$ cup mango chutney

1 tablespoon dark sesame oil

1 $^{1}/_{2}$ tablespoons curry powder

$^{1}/_{4}$ teaspoon salt

$^{1}/_{4}$ teaspoon freshly ground black pepper

1. Put the almonds in a small, nonstick skillet and cook, stirring frequently, over medium heat until fragrant and toasted, about 5 minutes. Set aside.

2. Combine all the salad ingredients, except the toasted almonds, in a large bowl.

3. Combine all the dressing ingredients in a blender or food processor and purée. Pour the dressing into the salad and toss well. Cover and refrigerate until cold. Stir in the almonds or sprinkle them over the top just before serving.

Makes eight 1 $^{1}/_{4}$-cup servings

Each serving contains approximately
Calories: 328
Fat: 9 g
Cholesterol: 48 mg
Sodium: 335 mg

Stuffed Bell Peppers

ᴈ

You can substitute ground chicken or beef for the turkey in this recipe. You can also use the filling to stuff other vegetables or cook it separately and serve it as a topping on pasta or beans.

---

4 large green bell peppers
1 pound ground turkey
1 medium-size onion, finely chopped
$\frac{1}{2}$ cup raw instant brown rice
1 $\frac{1}{2}$ teaspoons Italian herb blend, crushed
$\frac{1}{4}$ teaspoon salt
$\frac{1}{4}$ teaspoon freshly ground black pepper
One 8-ounce can tomato sauce
$\frac{1}{2}$ cup dry red wine
$\frac{1}{4}$ cup freshly grated Parmesan cheese

1. Slice the stem end off each bell pepper. Carefully remove and discard the seeds and membranes inside of the peppers. Set the bell peppers aside.

2. Combine the turkey, onion, rice, Italian herb blend, salt, pepper, and half of the tomato sauce in a medium-size bowl and mix well.

3. Spoon the mixture into the hollowed out peppers and place them, upright, in a medium-size saucepan. Combine the remaining tomato sauce and wine and pour over the stuffed peppers.

4. Bring the liquid to a boil over medium-high heat. Reduce the heat to low and simmer, covered, until the peppers are tender, about 45 minutes.

5. To serve, place one stuffed pepper on each of four plates and spoon a little of the liquid over the top. Sprinkle 1 tablespoon of the Parmesan cheese over each serving.

Makes 4 servings

Each serving contains approximately
Calories: 310
Fat: 11 g
Cholesterol: 88 mg
Sodium: 717 mg

Meatloaf in an Onion

⌘

Leave it to Dian Thomas, the television personality and author who teaches us about camping and outdoor cooking, to come up with this innovative, satisfying, and healthy meal for outdoor-cooking enthusiasts.

"But you don't have to stand out in the cold to barbecue," she says. "In the winter, use your fireplace. After all, this is how people cooked before there were ovens!"

1 pound very lean ground beef
2 large egg whites
¼ cup tomato sauce
⅛ teaspoon freshly ground black pepper
½ teaspoon salt
½ teaspoon dry mustard
6 medium-size onions

1. Cut six 12 × 14-inch rectangles of heavy aluminum foil and set aside.

2. In a medium-size bowl, combine the beef, egg whites, tomato sauce, pepper, salt, and dry mustard. Mix well and set aside.

3. Peel the onions and cut them in half horizontally. Remove the centers, leaving a ¼-inch shell. Finely chop the center from one of the onions and mix it into the meat mixture. Tightly wrap the 5 remaining onion centers and refrigerate for future use.

4. Spoon the meat mixture into 6 of the onion halves, mounding it on top. Place the remaining onion halves on top of the filled halves and press together. Place one filled onion on top of each piece of foil. Bring the ends of the foil up over the onion and fold down tightly in small folds. Flatten the ends and roll them tightly around the onion.

5. Cook the stuffed onions on coals, turning once, until they are soft to the touch, 14 to 20 minutes on each side. You can also bake them in a preheated 350° F oven for 45 minutes.

Makes 6 servings

Each serving contains approximately
Calories: 292
Fat: 16 g
Cholesterol: 57 mg
Sodium: 334 mg

Soups,
Stews, and
Sautés

Potato Jack Soup

ॐ

This recipe is a revision of a restaurant recipe from a reader in Lawrenceville, New Jersey. The original version of this truly tasty soup contained 411 calories, 87 milligrams of cholesterol, and 30 grams of fat per serving!

---

1 $1/2$ teaspoons corn-oil margarine
1 small white onion, chopped (1 cup)
5 cups fat-free chicken stock
1 bay leaf
$1/4$ teaspoon hot sauce
$1/4$ teaspoon freshly ground black pepper
$1/8$ teaspoon dried marjoram, crushed
1 $1/2$ pounds red potatoes, unpeeled, scrubbed, and quartered
4 ounces reduced-fat Monterey Jack cheese, grated (1 cup)
$1/4$ cup nonfat cream cheese
2 ounces reduced-fat sharp Cheddar cheese, grated ($1/2$ cup)

1. Melt the margarine in a large saucepan over medium-low heat. Add the onion and cook, stirring occasionally, until tender but not brown, about 5 minutes. Add the stock, bay leaf, hot sauce, pepper, and marjoram. Increase the heat to high and bring to a boil.

2. Add the potatoes to the pan of boiling stock. Reduce the heat to low and simmer until the potatoes are soft, about 25 minutes. Remove the pan from the heat and strain the solids, saving both the solids and the stock. Remove the bay leaf and discard.

3. Fill a blender container half full with the strained solids. Add about 2 cups of the stock and blend until smooth; pour into the same saucepan. Repeat the procedure until all the soup is blended.

4. Add the Jack cheese and cream cheese to the pan and cook over low heat, stirring constantly, until the cheese is melted, about 5 minutes.

5. Ladle the soup into 1-cup serving bowls. Top each portion with 1 tablespoon Cheddar cheese. Serve immediately.

Makes eight 1-cup servings

Each serving contains approximately
Calories: 151
Fat: 7 g
Cholesterol: 17 mg
Sodium: 213 mg

Black Olive and Clam Soup

ૐ

This delightful and unusual soup is based on a recipe created by Jean-Louis Palladin for Palladin, his new restaurant in The Watergate Hotel in Washington, D.C. In revising his original recipe, I changed the ratio of olives to potatoes a bit to lower the overall fat content of each serving. Even though olives are a fruit that is high in fat, the fat is monounsaturated, which tends to lower the "bad" cholesterol while increasing the "good" cholesterol.

Jean-Louis made this soup with Niçoise olives and served it over red-mullet fillets. I have called for Kalamata olives in this recipe because they are available pitted and the Niçoise are not. And because red-mullet fillets are often difficult to find, I have used canned clams, which are readily available and wonderful with the other flavors in the recipe.

On the other hand, I have retained Jean-Louis's unusual step of baking the potatoes instead of boiling them—even though it takes an hour. The resulting flavor and texture are worth the wait. I suggest serving this soup with whole-wheat toast or rolls.

2 medium-size (10 ounces) russet potatoes, unpeeled and scrubbed
One 4 ½-ounce jar pitted Kalamata olives, drained
Two 8-ounce bottles clam juice
Two 6 ½-ounce cans chopped clams, undrained
¼ teaspoon freshly ground black pepper
1 tablespoon freshly grated lemon zest, plus additional, for garnish
   (optional)
4 plum tomatoes, peeled and finely diced (1 cup)

1. Preheat the oven to 400° F.

2. Bake the potatoes in the preheated oven until soft when pierced with a knife, about 1 hour. Remove from the oven and allow to cool before handling. Cut into halves and scoop out the potato pulp and set it aside. Either discard the potato skins or save them for future use.

3. Combine the olives and clam juice in a medium-size saucepan. Drain the canned clams, reserving the juice. Add the juice to the pan and bring to a boil over medium heat. Reduce the heat to low and simmer for 5 minutes to let the flavors blend.

4. Allow the olive mixture to cool slightly. Pour it into a blender or food processor and purée. Add the reserved potato pulp and the pepper and blend until completely smooth. Pour the mixture through a sieve back into the pan. Stir in the 1 tablespoon lemon zest and heat to the desired temperature.

5. To serve, place one-quarter of the diced tomato in the bottom of each of four bowls. Add one-quarter of the drained clams to each bowl. Pour 1 cup of the soup over the tomato and clams in each bowl. Garnish with the additional lemon zest if desired.

Makes 4 servings

Each serving contains approximately
Calories: 150
Fat: 3 g
Cholesterol: 46 mg
Sodium: 757 mg

French Onion and Oyster Soup

⁊

**This hearty soup with toasted French bread makes a
satisfying meal on a cold winter day.**

---

1 tablespoon corn-oil margarine
2 large onions, thinly sliced (4 cups)
*1 pint shucked Maryland oysters with their liquid; or two 8-ounce
    cans, undrained*
4 cups fat-free chicken stock
¼ cup sherry
½ teaspoon Worcestershire sauce
4 ounces reduced-fat Swiss cheese, grated (1 cup)
¼ cup freshly grated Parmesan cheese
8 thin slices toasted French bread

1. Melt the margarine in a large, heavy saucepan over medium heat.
Add the onions and cook, stirring frequently, until tender but not
brown, about 5 minutes. Add the oysters and any juice. Cook until the
edges start to curl. (If you use canned oysters, you do not need to
cook them until their edges curl because they are already cooked;

just add the canned oysters and all the liquid from the cans and proceed with the recipe.)

2. Add the stock, sherry, and Worcestershire sauce and continue to cook over low heat until the mixture is hot.

3. To serve, spoon 1 cup of the soup into each of eight bowls and top each serving with 2 tablespoons of the Swiss cheese and ½ table-spoon of the Parmesan cheese. Top each bowl with a thin slice of the toasted bread.

Makes eight 1-cup servings

Each serving contains approximately
Calories: 135
Fat: 6 g
Cholesterol: 44 mg
Sodium: 182 mg

Smoked Chicken, Broccoli, and Black Bean Soup

ᴈ

This soup is even better if you can make it a day ahead of time and allow the flavors to "marry" overnight in the refrigerator.

1 tablespoon corn-oil margarine
$^{1}/_{2}$ cup each diced carrots, onions, and celery
1 cup peeled and diced broccoli stems
2 teaspoons dried thyme, crushed
2 teaspoons dried oregano, crushed
1 teaspoon dried basil, crushed
$^{1}/_{4}$ cup dry white wine
4 cups fat-free chicken stock, hot
1 tablespoon Worcestershire sauce
$^{1}/_{2}$ teaspoon Tabasco
6 ounces boneless, skinless, smoked chicken breast, diced (1 cup)
1 cup cooked black beans, drained and rinsed if canned
1 cup broccoli florets
2 cups low-fat (2 percent) milk
2 tablespoons light cream cheese
$^{1}/_{4}$ teaspoon salt (omit if using salted stock)
$^{1}/_{4}$ teaspoon freshly ground black pepper

1. Melt the margarine in a large saucepan or soup kettle over medium heat. Add the carrots, onion, celery, and broccoli stems and cook, stirring, for 5 minutes. Add the thyme, oregano, and basil and cook, stirring, about 5 minutes more.

2. Add the wine and bring to a boil over medium heat, scraping up any browned bits in the pan. Add the stock and cook until reduced by one-third, about 10 minutes. (You should have about 3 ½ cups mixture remaining.) Reduce the heat to low, add the Worcestershire sauce, Tabasco, smoked chicken breast, beans, and broccoli florets, and simmer for 5 minutes.

3. Add the milk and cream cheese and simmer, stirring, 5 minutes more. Stir in salt and pepper.

Makes four 1 ½-cup servings

Each serving contains approximately
Calories: **283**
Fat: **9 g**
Cholesterol: **39 mg**
Sodium: **431 mg**

Beef and Black Bean Soup

ॐ

For one of my "bean of the month" columns a few years ago, I ran this recipe created by Terryl Propper, an endodontist (a dentist who specializes in root-canal treatment) in Nashville, Tennessee. She won first place in her state competition with this soup and was selected one of the top fifteen finalists in the country to compete in the National Beef Cook-Off. Even though Terryl did not win the Best of Beef award, her quick, easy, economical, and really delicious stew-type soup was my favorite entry. She suggests serving it with corn tortillas.

1 pound coarsely ground beef chuck
One 11-ounce can black bean soup
One 15-ounce can black beans, rinsed and drained
1 ⅓ cups water
1 cup prepared medium or hot chunky salsa
¼ cup thinly sliced green onions (scallions), including green tops
¼ cup light sour cream, for garnish
Fresh cilantro sprigs, for garnish

1. Cook the beef in a 2- or 3-quart saucepan over medium heat until no longer pink, about 3 minutes. Stir frequently while cooking to break it up into ¾-inch crumbles. Pour off any drippings.

2. Stir in the soup, beans, water, and salsa. Bring to a boil over medium-high heat and then reduce the heat to low and simmer, uncovered, for 15 minutes.

3. Remove the pan from the heat and stir in the green onions. Garnish with the sour cream and cilantro.

Makes four 1 ¼-cup servings

Each serving contains approximately
Calories: 446
Fat: 17 g
Cholesterol: 92 mg
Sodium: 208 mg

Cider-Braised Red Cabbage with Bacon and Beans

ॐ

Cabbage, along with broccoli, cauliflower, Brussels sprouts, and kohlrabi, is a cruciferous vegetable. The name refers to their cross-shaped flowers. According to the American Cancer Society, eating these vegetables regularly can actually help to prevent certain types of cancer. For this reason, it makes good sense to work these wonderful vegetables into our menus as often as possible.

This vegetable stew is both delicious and extremely versatile. It can be served hot or cold.

1 medium-size onion, thinly sliced (2 cups)
6 ounces Canadian bacon, cut into matchstick strips (about ³/₄ cups)
1 tablespoon dark brown sugar
¹/₄ cup red wine vinegar
1 cup fat-free chicken stock
¹/₂ cup apple cider or juice
¹/₄ teaspoon salt (omit if using salted stock)
¹/₄ teaspoon freshly ground black pepper
1 small head red cabbage (1 pound), cored and thinly sliced (6 cups)

1 tablespoon extra-virgin olive oil
One 15-ounce can cannellini beans, drained and rinsed

1. In a large saucepan, combine the onion and Canadian bacon. Cook, covered, over low heat until the onion is tender but not browned, about 10 to 15 minutes. Add a little water if necessary to prevent scorching.

2. Add the brown sugar and continue cooking until well blended. Add the vinegar, stock, cider or juice, salt, and pepper and mix well. Add the cabbage and again mix well. Simmer over low heat, covered, for 15 minutes. Uncover and bring to a rapid boil over high heat. Continue to boil until the pan is almost dry, about 15 minutes.

3. Drain any remaining liquid. Add the olive oil and beans and mix well. Serve hot or refrigerate and serve cold.

Makes four 1 ½-cup servings

Each serving contains approximately
Calories: 241
Fat: 8 g
Cholesterol: 25 mg
Sodium: 984 mg

Bouillabaisse

⌐

This flavorful, aromatic fish stew was originally created by the fishermen in Marseilles, on the southern coast of France. They used whatever fish and seafood they had not sold to make their stew, so the ingredients varied from one day to another. The spice saffron, however, was a constant. Even though it is expensive, it is an essential ingredient for an authentic bouillabaisse. Serve this hearty dish with plenty of crusty French bread.

1 tablespoon extra-virgin olive oil
2 medium-size onions, finely chopped (3 cups)
2 cloves garlic, pressed or minced
One 8-ounce bottle clam juice
2 cups dry white wine
One 14 1/2-ounce can ready-cut tomatoes, undrained
*1 small bulb fennel, trimmed and finely chopped, including the
    fern (2 cups)*
2 tablespoons chopped fresh parsley
1 bay leaf
1/2 teaspoon dried thyme, crushed
1/4 teaspoon saffron

¼ teaspoon freshly ground black pepper
8 ounces firm whitefish fillets, cubed (2 cups)
8 ounces sea scallops

1. Heat the olive oil in a large, flameproof casserole over medium heat. Add the onions and garlic and cook, stirring frequently, until tender but not browned, about 5 minutes. Add all the remaining ingredients except the fish and scallops and bring to a boil over medium heat. Reduce the heat to low and simmer, uncovered, for 15 minutes. Add the fish and scallops and continue to cook until they turn from translucent to opaque, about 2 minutes more.

2. To serve, divide the fish and scallops equally into four bowls and spoon the soup over the top.

Makes 4 servings

Each serving contains approximately
Calories: 286
Fat: 7 g
Cholesterol: 42 mg
Sodium: 810 mg

Venetian Chicken with Beans and Bacon

∿

If you don't have any Canadian bacon or if you just
want to eliminate one step in this recipe, you can leave
out the bacon and get a similar smoky flavor by adding
$\frac{1}{2}$ teaspoon of liquid smoke when you add the beans.

---

1 tablespoon extra-virgin olive oil

3 ounces Canadian bacon, diced (about 6 slices)

4 boneless, skinless chicken breast halves, cut lengthwise into
    1-inch strips

$\frac{1}{4}$ teaspoon freshly ground black pepper

1 clove garlic, minced

1 medium-size onion, finely chopped (1 $\frac{1}{2}$ cups)

2 ribs celery, finely chopped ($\frac{1}{2}$ cup)

$\frac{1}{2}$ cup dry white wine

2 teaspoons finely chopped fresh thyme; or $\frac{1}{2}$ teaspoon dried
    thyme, crushed

$\frac{1}{2}$ teaspoon finely chopped fresh rosemary; or $\frac{1}{2}$ teaspoon dried
    rosemary, crushed

Two 15-ounce cans cannellini beans, undrained
4 plum tomatoes, peeled and diced
2 tablespoons finely chopped fresh parsley
Freshly grated Parmesan cheese (optional)

1. Heat the olive oil in a large, heavy skillet over medium heat. Add the bacon and cook, stirring frequently, for 3 minutes. Add the chicken and continue to stir-fry until it has lost its pink color and is completely opaque, 3 to 4 minutes more. Remove the chicken from the skillet and set aside.

2. Add the pepper, garlic, onion, and celery to the skillet and continue to cook, stirring frequently, over medium heat until the onion is tender but not browned, about 5 minutes. Add the wine and and cook until reduced by half, about 3 minutes. Add the thyme, rosemary, and beans and bring to a simmer. Add the chicken and simmer for 5 more minutes.

3. To serve, spoon 1 ½ cups of the mixture onto each of four plates. Top each serving with one-quarter of the tomato and a sprinkle of the parsley. If desired, top with a little Parmesan cheese.

Makes four 1 ½-cup servings

Each serving contains approximately
Calories: 412
Fat: 9 g
Cholesterol: 83 mg
Sodium: 915 mg

Sautéed Chicken, Olives, and Bell Peppers with Lemon Couscous

✌

The culinary philosophy of the Seabourn Cruise Line is to always include regional-style dishes using local ingredients along with their highly acclaimed international gourmet cuisine. When we were cruising in the Greek Islands on the *Seabourn Spirit,* the executive chef, Harald Markt, served this sensational dish.

Lemon Couscous
2 cups fat-free chicken stock
1/4 teaspoon salt (omit if using salted stock)
1/4 teaspoon freshly ground black pepper
1 teaspoon grated lemon zest
2 tablespoons fresh lemon juice
2 teaspoons extra-virgin olive oil
1 cup (6 3/4 ounces) couscous

1 tablespoon extra-virgin olive oil
4 whole chicken legs, including the thighs, skin removed

1 onion, coarsely chopped
1 red bell pepper, seeds and membranes removed, chopped
1 green bell pepper, seeds and membranes removed, chopped
8 small Kalamata olives, pitted and halved
¼ cup dry red wine
¼ cup fat-free chicken stock
1 bay leaf
½ teaspoon dried thyme, crushed
¼ teaspoon dried rosemary, crushed
¼ teaspoon salt
¼ teaspoon freshly ground black pepper
3 plum tomatoes, peeled and diced

1. To make the lemon couscous, combine all the ingredients except the couscous in a medium-size saucepan with a tight-fitting lid. Bring to a boil, uncovered, over medium-high heat and remove from the heat. Stir in the couscous, cover tightly, and allow to stand for 5 minutes. Uncover and fluff the couscous with a fork.

2. Heat the olive oil in a large, nonstick skillet. Add the chicken and cook until lightly browned on both sides, about 10 minutes.

3. Add the onion, bell peppers, and olives and cook, covered, over low heat until the onion is soft and translucent, 15 to 20 minutes. Add the wine, stock, bay leaf, thyme, rosemary, salt, and pepper. Simmer over low heat, uncovered, for 10 minutes. Add the tomatoes and continue to simmer for 5 more minutes.

4. To serve, spoon ¾ cup of the lemon couscous on each of four plates and top with a chicken leg and 1 cup of the sauce from the skillet.

Makes 4 servings

Each serving contains approximately
Calories: 499
Fat: 17 g
Cholesterol: 107 mg
Sodium: 344 mg

Chicken Cacciatore with Linguini

ᔒ

The original recipe for this dish called for ¼ cup of oil, which is totally unnecessary. I prefer to spray the chicken pieces with the oil rather than spraying the pan because it beads up on the surface of a nonstick pan and does not evenly crisp the chicken. You can do this with either a can of nonstick vegetable spray or by putting some extra-virgin olive oil in a spray bottle that you can buy in any market.

½ cup unbleached all-purpose flour
½ teaspoon salt
½ teaspoon freshly ground black pepper
4 whole skinless chicken legs, including the thighs
¼ pound white mushrooms, sliced (1 cup)
1 medium-size onion, chopped (1 ½ cups)
1 small green bell pepper, seeds and membranes removed,
    chopped (1 cup)
1 clove garlic, pressed or minced
One 28-ounce can chopped tomatoes, undrained
½ cup dry white wine

³/₄ teaspoon dried thyme, crushed
³/₄ teaspoon dried oregano, crushed
1 bay leaf
12 ounces linguini pasta, cooked al dente

1. Combine the flour, salt, and pepper in a plastic bag. Add the chicken and shake until well coated. Lightly spray the chicken pieces with olive oil. Heat a large, nonstick skillet over medium heat. Add the chicken and cook until lightly browned on both sides, about 10 minutes. Remove the chicken from the skillet and set aside. Add the mushrooms, onion, green pepper, and garlic to the skillet and cook, stirring frequently, until the onion is tender, about 5 minutes.

2. Stir in the tomatoes, wine, thyme, oregano, and bay leaf. Cook over medium heat, stirring frequently until the mixture comes to a full boil. Add the chicken and cover. Reduce the heat to low and simmer until the chicken is tender, 30 minutes. Remove the bay leaf.

3. To serve, spoon 1 cup of the linguini on each of four plates. Top the pasta with a chicken leg and spoon the sauce equally over the top of each serving.

Makes 4 servings

Each serving contains approximately
Calories: 560
Fat: 13 g
Cholesterol: 93 mg
Sodium: 838 mg

Lamb Stew

~

This stew can be made with beef or pork instead of lamb if you prefer. Also, you can omit the potatoes and serve it over pasta or rice.

1 pound lean boneless lamb, cut into 1 $\frac{1}{2}$-inch cubes
$\frac{1}{4}$ cup unbleached all-purpose flour
$\frac{1}{2}$ teaspoon salt
$\frac{1}{4}$ teaspoon freshly ground black pepper
One 14 $\frac{1}{2}$-ounce can ready-cut tomatoes, undrained
$\frac{1}{4}$ cup dry red wine
1 medium onion, chopped (1 $\frac{1}{2}$ cups)
4 small carrots ($\frac{1}{2}$ pound), cut into 1-inch pieces
2 ribs celery, cut into 1-inch pieces
$\frac{1}{2}$ pound white mushrooms, sliced (2 cups)
1 green bell pepper, seeds and membranes removed, coarsely
    chopped (1 cup)
4 red potatoes (1 pound total), unpeeled, scrubbed, and cut into
    1-inch chunks
1 teaspoon dried basil, crushed
1 teaspoon dried oregano, crushed

1. Preheat the oven to 325° F.

2. Spray a 10-inch, nonstick skillet with nonstick vegetable spray and heat over medium-high heat. Sprinkle the lamb with 1 tablespoon of the flour and the salt and pepper. Place it in the skillet and brown, stirring constantly, on all sides, about 10 minutes. Transfer the browned lamb to a 3-quart casserole. Set aside.

3. To the skillet add the remaining flour along with the juice from the tomatoes and the wine. Mix well and cook over medium heat until thickened, about 10 minutes.

4. Pour the thickened sauce over the lamb. Add the tomatoes and onion to the lamb and mix well. Cover and bake in the preheated oven for 1 hour. Remove from the oven and stir in all the remaining ingredients. Cover and bake until all the vegetables are tender, another hour.

Makes 4 servings

Each serving contains approximately
Calories: 354
Fat: 9 g
Cholesterol: 75 mg
Sodium: 674 mg

Baked Beef Stew

ॐ

This easy-to-make stew recipe was sent to me by a reader. The addition of the tapioca is a bit unusual; it slightly thickens the sauce and gives the finished dish a very nice texture.

2 pounds lean round steak, cut into 1-inch cubes
1 ½ cups fat-free beef stock
½ cup dry red wine
2 cups sliced carrots
2 cups sliced celery
2 medium-size onions, quartered
2 cups cubed peeled potatoes
2 tablespoons Minute tapioca
½ teaspoon salt (omit if using salted stock)
½ teaspoon dried marjoram, crushed
½ teaspoon dried thyme, crushed
¼ teaspoon freshly ground black pepper
1 bay leaf

1. Preheat oven to 300° F.

2. Combine all the ingredients in a 4-quart casserole. Cover and bake in the preheated oven until the meat is tender, about 3 hours. Stir at the end of each hour. Remove the bay leaf and serve in big bowls with crusty bread.

Makes 8 servings

Each serving contains approximately
Calories: 240
Fat: 6 g
Cholesterol: 66 mg
Sodium: 281 mg

Burgundy Pot Roast

⟫

I like to serve this hearty and flavorful stew with a big green salad and crusty bread.

$^1/_2$ cup unbleached all-purpose flour
$^1/_2$ teaspoon freshly ground black pepper
One 3-pound round-bone pot roast, all visible fat removed
1 teaspoon canola oil
1 cup Burgundy or another dry red wine
1 cup sherry
3 cups fat-free beef stock
$^1/_2$ teaspoon dried thyme, crushed
$^1/_4$ teaspoon dried marjoram, crushed
$^1/_4$ teaspoon dried basil, crushed
2 bay leaves
8 small new potatoes, unpeeled and scrubbed
4 medium-size carrots, peeled and halved
16 boiling onions; or 3 medium-size onions, quartered
2 cups frozen peas, thawed

1. Combine the flour and pepper in a medium-size plastic bag. Add the roast and shake until well coated, patting off any excess flour.

2. Heat the oil in a large, heavy skillet or Dutch oven over medium heat. Add the floured roast and brown, turning frequently until well browned on both sides, about 20 minutes. Add the wine and simmer until almost dry. Add the sherry and again simmer until almost dry. Add the stock, thyme, marjoram, basil, and bay leaves and simmer, covered, over low heat, for 1 ½ hours. Add the potatoes, carrots, and onions and simmer until tender, about 30 minutes. Add the peas during the last 5 minutes of cooking.

Makes 8 servings

Each serving contains approximately
Calories: 336
Fat: 11 g
Cholesterol: 88 mg
Sodium: 194 mg

Quick-and-Easy Osso Bucco Stew

⁊

This new take on a classic was sent to me by one of my readers. It is certainly easy to make and is truly delicious.

2 teaspoons olive oil
3 cloves garlic, pressed or minced
2 pounds sliced veal shank (4 slices), all visible fat removed
1 cup dry red wine
One 14 1/2-ounce can ready-cut tomatoes, undrained
3 medium-size onions, chopped (4 1/2 cups)
1 tablespoon dried oregano, crushed
1/2 teaspoon dried rosemary, crushed
1 bay leaf
1/4 teaspoon salt
1/2 teaspoon freshly ground black pepper
1 bulb fennel, including the fern, coarsely chopped (3 cups)
8 small new potatoes, unpeeled and scrubbed
2 teaspoons grated lemon zest
Italian parsley sprigs, for garnish

1. Heat the olive oil in a large skillet or Dutch oven over medium heat. Add the garlic and cook until it sizzles. Add the veal shanks and cook until well browned on both sides, about 20 minutes.

2. Add ½ cup of the wine and cook until almost dry. Add the remaining wine, tomatoes, onions, oregano, rosemary, bay leaf, salt, and pepper and simmer, covered, over low heat for 1 ½ hours.

3. Add the fennel and potatoes and cook until tender, about 30 more minutes. Uncover and continue cooking until the sauce thickens.

4. To serve, place a slice of the veal shank on each of four plates. Spoon the vegetables and sauce over the top, sprinkle each serving with lemon zest, and garnish with a parsley sprig.

Makes 4 servings

Each serving contains approximately
Calories: 347
Fat: 14 g
Cholesterol: 88 mg
Sodium: 500 mg

Cajun Smothered Pork Chops

⌖

The Cajun word for this dish is *maquechoux*, which means "smothered with corn." In this recipe I have called for both canned cream-style corn and corn kernels. For the kernels, you can use fresh, frozen, or salt-free canned corn, drained.

---

1 medium-size onion, finely chopped (1 ½ cups)
2 ribs celery, finely chopped (½ cup)
1 small bell pepper, seeds and membranes removed, finely
    chopped (¾ cup)
One 14 ½-ounce can ready-cut tomatoes, undrained
½ teaspoon freshly ground black pepper
½ teaspoon dried basil, crushed
½ teaspoon dried thyme, crushed
½ teaspoon dried tarragon, crushed
⅛ teaspoon cayenne pepper, or to taste
4 lean pork chops, all visible fat removed (1 pound meat)
¼ cup dry white wine
One 15-ounce can unsalted cream-style corn kernels
1 cup corn kernels

1. Combine the onion, celery, bell pepper, tomatoes, pepper, basil, thyme, tarragon, and cayenne pepper in a large saucepan or Dutch oven and cook, covered, over low heat for 20 minutes, stirring occasionally.

2. While the vegetable mixture is cooking, cook the pork chops in a large, nonstick skillet over medium heat until well browned on both sides, about 10 minutes. Add the wine and cook, covered, for 10 more minutes. Uncover and cook over high heat until most of the wine is absorbed, about 3 minutes.

3. Add the cream-style corn and the corn kernels to the vegetable mixture and mix well. Bury the browned pork chops in the mixture and add any liquid still in the pork pan. Simmer, covered, over low heat for 15 more minutes to allow the flavors to blend.

4. To serve, place 1 pork chop on each of four plates or shallow bowls and spoon 1 cup of the corn mixture over the top.

Makes 4 servings

Each serving contains approximately
Calories: 397
Fat: 15 g
Cholesterol: 81 mg
Sodium: 314 mg

Pasta

Pasta Primavera with Dried-Tomato Sauce

⅋

In this recipe I call for a rotini-cut pasta because the grooves in its spiral shape help to hold the sauce better than most other types of pasta. But you can certainly use any other pasta cut (fresh or dry) of your choice and either mix the sauce with it or, if you prefer, serve the sauce over the top.

One 10 ³/₄-ounce can low-fat condensed cream of mushroom soup
One 12-ounce can evaporated skim milk
²/₃ cup dried tomato bits
¹/₄ teaspoon freshly ground black pepper
2 cloves garlic, pressed or minced; or ¹/₄ teaspoon garlic powder
¹/₈ teaspoon ground nutmeg
¹/₂ teaspoon dried oregano, crushed
1 teaspoon dried thyme, crushed
One 16-ounce package frozen mixed vegetables, thawed
8 ounces rotini pasta, cooked al dente
¹/₂ cup freshly grated Parmesan cheese

1. Combine the mushroom soup and skim milk in a large saucepan and mix well. Add the dried tomatoes, pepper, garlic, nutmeg, oregano, and thyme and bring to a boil over medium heat. Reduce the heat to low and cook, stirring frequently, for 5 minutes. Stir in the vegetables and heat through.

2. Remove the pan from the heat and stir in the cooked pasta. Top each serving with 2 tablespoons of the grated cheese.

Makes four 2-cup servings

Each serving contains approximately
Calories: 448
Fat: 7 g
Cholesterol: 16 mg
Sodium: 702 mg

Whole-Wheat Pasta with Fresh Vegetables

᧡

This delicious and colorful pasta dish was created by Jerry Peters, the talented executive chef at Enchantment Resort in Sedona, Arizona. I was delighted to learn that this wonderfully nutritious, high-fiber vegetarian entree is the best-selling pasta dish on the menu.

If you don't have some of the vegetables called for in the recipe, just substitute what you do have and create your own spur-of-the-moment version of this popular dish.

---

8 ounces whole-wheat pasta
1 cup fat-free chicken stock
$^1/_2$ teaspoon salt (omit if using salted stock)
1 tablespoon extra-virgin olive oil
4 cloves garlic, pressed or minced
4 green onions (scallions), including green tops, bias cut into $^1/_2$-inch pieces (1 cup)
$^1/_2$ pound fresh asparagus, bias cut into $^1/_2$-inch pieces (1 cup)

¹/₄ pound white mushrooms, sliced (1 cup)
3 ripe plum tomatoes, quartered
¹/₄ cup fresh basil leaves, chopped
2 tablespoons fresh Italian parsley, chopped
Freshly ground black pepper to taste
Freshy grated Parmesan cheese to taste (optional)

1. Cook the pasta in a large pot of boiling water until tender but still very firm (not quite al dente), about 8 minutes. Drain thoroughly and return to the pot. Add the stock and, if using, the salt and simmer until most of the stock has been absorbed, 2 to 3 minutes.

2. While the pasta is cooking, heat the olive oil in a large skillet. Add the garlic, green onions, asparagus, and mushrooms and cook over medium-high heat, stirring constantly, until the asparagus is tender but still firm, 3 to 5 minutes. Add the tomatoes, basil, and parsley and toss well.

3. Add the vegetable mixture to the cooked pasta and toss thoroughly. Serve immediately, spooning 1 ½ cups of the mixture onto each of four plates. Top each serving with a little freshly ground black pepper and, if desired, Parmesan cheese.

Makes 4 servings

Each serving contains approximately
Calories: 250
Fat: 6 g
Cholesterol: 68 mg
Sodium: 345 mg

Fresh Creamed Corn with Red Pepper Pasta

ᔓ

This creamed-corn dish is best in the summertime when fresh corn is at its peak. I like to serve the sauce over red pepper pasta because it makes such a pretty and colorful presentation. It is, however, very good with any kind of pasta, rice, or beans you happen to have on hand.

---

4 ears fresh corn, husked
2 cups low-fat milk
¹/₂ large onion, coarsely chopped
¹/₂ teaspoon whole black peppercorns
¹/₄ cup unbleached all-purpose flour
¹/₂ teaspoon salt
1 pound fresh red pepper pasta

1. Cut the corn kernels off the cobs and place in a medium-size bowl. Standing each corn cob in the same bowl and using the dull side of a knife, scrape the cobs to "milk" the remaining liquid from each cob. Set the corn and corn "milk" aside. Reserve one of the scraped cobs and discard the others.

2. In a large, heavy saucepan, combine 1 ¾ cups of the milk, the onion, and the peppercorns. Break the reserved cob into halves and add it to the pan. Slowly bring the milk mixture to a boil. Reduce the heat to low and simmer, uncovered, for 5 minutes. Strain the mixture and discard the corn cob, onion, and peppercorns.

3. Pour the strained liquid back into the saucepan. In a small bowl, combine the remaining ¼ cup of milk with the flour and salt. Stir until the flour is completely dissolved and then add it to the saucepan. Bring the mixture back to a boil over medium heat and cook, stirring constantly, until the mixture has thickened, about 3 minutes. Add the reserved corn kernels and corn "milk" and continue cooking over low heat for 15 more minutes.

4. Cook the pasta in a large pot of boiling water until al dente, 2 to 3 minutes. Drain thoroughly and spoon 1 cup of it onto each of 6 plates. Top each serving with ½ cup of the creamed corn. Or stir the pasta into the corn mixture if you prefer.

Makes six ½-cup servings

Each serving contains approximately
Calories: 114
Fat: 2 g
Cholesterol: 7 mg
Sodium: 245 mg

Spinach Noodles with Three Cheeses

∻

I like the look of this dish best when it's made with green spinach noodles, but any type of pasta can be substituted.

2 tablespoons corn-oil margarine
3 tablespoons unbleached all-purpose flour
2 ½ cups nonfat milk, heated until bubbles appear around the edge
¼ teaspoon salt
¼ teaspoon freshly ground black pepper
⅛ teaspoon ground nutmeg
8 ounces spinach noodles
¾ cup plus 2 tablespoons freshly grated Parmesan cheese
4 ounces reduced-fat Swiss cheese, diced (¾ cup)
4 ounces part-skim mozzarella cheese, diced (¾ cup)

1. Preheat the oven to 350° F.

2. Melt 1 tablespoon of the margarine in a medium-size saucepan over low heat. Add the flour and cook, stirring constantly, for 2 minutes; do not brown. Remove the pan from the heat and add the

simmering milk slowly, stirring constantly with a wire whisk. Add the salt, pepper, and nutmeg. Return to low heat and cook, stirring frequently, until this white sauce thickens, about 30 minutes. Set aside.

3. While the sauce is cooking, cook the noodles in a large pot of boiling water until al dente. Drain well and toss with the remaining tablespoon of margarine, then with ¾ cup of the Parmesan cheese. Add the Swiss and mozzarella cheeses and toss lightly.

4. Turn half of the noodle mixture into a 9 × 13-inch or 3-quart baking dish sprayed with nonstick vegetable spray. Top with half the white sauce. Repeat the layers and sprinkle with the remaining 2 tablespoons of Parmesan cheese.

5. Bake in the preheated oven until bubbling, about 25 minutes.

Makes eight ⅔-cup servings

Each serving contains approximately
Calories: 261
Fat: 9 g
Cholesterol: 22 mg
Sodium: 372 mg

Pizzoccheri

ॐ

This hearty Italian peasant recipe was given to my newspaper column editor, Sandy Klink, by the people at Darien Fine Food and Cheese when she asked them what they did with their buckwheat pasta. She called me the next day raving about the dish and asked me if I could lighten it up enough for my column.

I am delighted to report that my revision uses only one-sixth of the fat called for in the original recipe without losing the integrity of the dish. I must admit, though, that this dish will never win any awards for appearance, so I recommend garnishing it with tomato wedges to add a bit of color.

2 bunches (2 pounds) fresh spinach, stems removed, thoroughly washed
1 medium-size head green cabbage, cut into strips
2 tablespoons corn-oil margarine
3 cloves garlic, pressed or minced
¼ cup extra-virgin olive oil
¼ teaspoon salt
¼ teaspoon freshly ground black pepper

1 pound buckwheat pasta
6 ounces freshly grated, imported Parmesan cheese
6 ounces freshly grated Fontina cheese
Tomato wedges, for garnish (optional)

1. Preheat the oven to 325° F.

2. Steam the spinach, covered, in a basket over simmering water until limp, about 3 minutes, and set aside. Steam the cabbage until limp, about 4 minutes, and set aside.

3. Melt the margarine in a small saucepan or skillet over medium heat. Add the garlic and cook until it sizzles. Remove from the heat and add the oil, salt, and pepper. Mix well and set aside.

4. Cook the pasta in boiling water until al dente, 8 to 10 minutes. Drain thoroughly and set aside.

5. In a large, ovenproof bowl, drizzle a little of the olive oil mixture. Add one-third of the pasta. Top with half of the spinach and cabbage. Then top with half of the Parmesan and Fontina cheeses. Repeat layering until all the ingredients are in the bowl and then gently toss them together.

6. Place the bowl in the preheated oven until the cheese melts, about 5 minutes. To serve, spoon the pasta mixture onto heated plates or bowls and garnish, if desired, with the tomato wedges.

Makes eight 2 ¼-cup servings

Each serving contains approximately
Calories: 453
Fat: 23 g
Cholesterol: 39 mg
Sodium: 675 mg

Lasagna Primavera

⁊

This is a delicious variation on traditional lasagna. Leftovers are good served cold and make a great picnic or brown-bag lunch dish.

1 $\frac{1}{2}$ cups fat-free chicken stock
One 12-ounce can evaporated skim milk
3 tablespoons corn-oil margarine
1 medium-size onion, thinly sliced
3 tablespoons all-purpose flour
$\frac{1}{4}$ teaspoon salt (omit if using salted stock)
$\frac{1}{4}$ teaspoon freshly ground black pepper
$\frac{1}{2}$ teaspoon dried oregano, crushed
$\frac{3}{4}$ teaspoon dried rosemary, crushed
1 $\frac{1}{2}$ teaspoons dried thyme, crushed
4 cups assorted colorful vegetables, in bite-size pieces, steamed
   crisp-tender
$\frac{1}{2}$ cup finely chopped fresh parsley
$\frac{1}{2}$ pound lasagna noodles, cooked al dente
One 15-ounce carton fat-free ricotta cheese
8 ounces reduced-fat sharp Cheddar cheese, grated (2 cups)
$\frac{1}{2}$ cup fresh whole-wheat bread crumbs (1 slice ground)

1. Preheat the oven to 350° F.

2. Combine the stock and milk and heat on top of the stove or in a microwave oven until bubbles appear around the edge, and set aside. Melt the margarine in 2- or 3-quart saucepan over medium-low heat. Add the onion and cook, covered, over low heat until the onion is translucent. Add a little water if necessary to prevent scorching. Add the flour and cook, stirring constantly for 2 minutes. Add the hot stock and milk mixture all at once, stirring constantly with a wire whisk. Bring to a boil over medium heat, reduce heat to low and simmer, stirring frequently, until the mixture starts to thicken, about 5 minutes. Remove from the heat and add the salt, pepper, oregano, rosemary, and thyme and mix well. Stir in the vegetables and parsley and set aside.

3. Spray a 9 × 13-inch baking dish with nonstick vegetable spray. Spread one-quarter of the vegetable mixture evenly over the bottom of the dish. Cover with a layer of the cooked lasagna noodles. Top the noodles with all the ricotta cheese and one-third of the remaining vegetable mixture. Add a second layer of noodles. Cover them with half of the remaining vegetable mixture. Sprinkle half of the Cheddar cheese evenly over the top. Top with the remaining noodles, vegetable mixture, and Cheddar cheese. Sprinkle the bread crumbs evenly over the top.

4. Bake, uncovered, in the preheated oven until bubbling and lightly browned, 30 minutes. Allow to stand for 5 minutes before cutting into eight approximately 3 × 4-inch servings.

Makes 8 servings

Each serving contains approximately
Calories: 453
Fat: 23 g
Cholestrol: 39 mg
Sodium: 675 mg

Southwestern White Lima Bean Lasagna

⟋

If you're planning a summer wedding and looking for a glamorous, relatively inexpensive, and completely vegetarian menu to serve, you might want to consider this one-dish Southwestern lasagna.

---

1 ½ cups vegetable stock
One 12-ounce can evaporated skim milk
2 tablespoons corn-oil margarine
3 cloves garlic, pressed or minced
1 large onion, finely chopped (2 cups)
3 tablespoons all-purpose flour
½ teaspoon salt (omit if using salted stock)
½ teaspoon freshly ground black pepper
2 teaspoons ground cumin
1 ½ teaspoons dry oregano, crushed
1 teaspoon ground coriander
¼ teaspoon ground cloves
¼ teaspoon cayenne pepper
4 cups cooked baby white lima beans
One 4-ounce can diced green chilies

8 ounces lasagna noodles, cooked al dente
One 15-ounce carton fat-free ricotta cheese
8 ounces shredded part-skim mozzarella cheese
3 corn tortillas, ground into crumbs (3 ounces = ½ cup crumbs)

1. Preheat the oven to 350° F. Spray a 9 × 13-inch baking dish with nonstick vegetable spray and set aside.

2. Combine the stock and milk and heat until bubbles appear around the edge either in a microwave or on top of the stove. Meanwhile, melt the margarine in a large saucepan or soup kettle over medium-low heat. Add the garlic and cook until it sizzles. Add the onion and cook until soft. Add the flour and cook, stirring constantly, for 2 minutes. Add the hot stock mixture, all at once, stirring constantly with a whisk. Bring to a boil, reduce heat to low and continue cooking, stirring frequently, for 10 minutes. Remove from the heat and stir in the salt, pepper, cumin, oregano, coriander, cloves, cayenne pepper, lima beans, and chilies.

3. Spread one-quarter of the bean mixture evenly over the bottom of the prepared baking dish. Top with a layer of the cooked noodles. Top the noodles with all the ricotta cheese and one-third of the remaining bean mixture. Add another layer of noodles and top them with half of the mozzarella and half of the remaining bean mixture. Top with the remaining noodles, bean mixture, and mozzarella. Sprinkle the tortilla crumbs evenly over the top of the dish.

4. Place in the preheated oven and bake, uncovered, until bubbly and lightly browned, 30 minutes. Remove from the oven and allow to stand for 5 minutes before cutting.

Makes 8 servings

Each serving contains approximately
Calories: 439
Fat: 9 g
Cholesterol: 24 mg
Sodium: 619 mg

Corn Lasagna

ॐ

This is a really quick and easy recipe using the new lasagna noodles that don't have to be boiled before baking.

---

6 ounces part-skim mozzarella cheese, grated (1 $\frac{1}{2}$ cups)
One 10-ounce package frozen corn kernels, thawed
One 15-ounce container nonfat ricotta cheese
2 large egg whites, lightly beaten
1 teaspoon dried oregano, crushed
1 teaspoon salt
$\frac{1}{4}$ teaspoon freshly ground black pepper
One 27 $\frac{1}{2}$-ounce jar low-fat spaghetti sauce
6 ounces (about 9) oven-ready lasagna noodles, uncooked
1 cup water

1. Preheat the oven to 325° F. Spray a 9 × 13-inch baking dish with nonstick vegetable spray and set aside.

2. Combine $\frac{1}{2}$ cup of the mozzarella cheese, the corn, ricotta, egg whites, oregano, salt, and pepper in a bowl and mix well.

3. Line the bottom of the prepared dish with about ¾ cup of the spaghetti sauce. Place half the noodles on top of the sauce. Top the noodles with half of the corn mixture. Top with the remaining noodles and remaining corn mixture. Pour the remaining spaghetti sauce over the top. Carefully pour the water around the edges and sprinkle with the remaining cup of mozzarella cheese.

4. Tightly cover the pan with foil and bake for 1 hour and 15 minutes. Let it rest 10 to 15 minutes before serving.

Makes 8 servings

Each serving contains approximately
Calories: 249
Fat: 5 g
Cholesterol: 18 mg
Sodium: 756 mg

Macheroni alla Pescatore

ॐ

When I was in Baltimore recently I was fortunate enough to meet and share a late lunch with Frank Velleggia, the owner of Casa de Pasta. The famous restaurant was started by his father, Enrico, and many of the dishes served are still made using the recipes brought over by his mother, "Miss Mary," from their native town in Italy.

My favorite dish on their menu was this sensational seafood pasta. Frank was kind enough to give me the recipe so that I could share it with my readers.

---

¹/₂ cup dry white wine
¹/₂ cup water
1 medium-size onion, finely chopped (1 ¹/₂ cups)
12 mussels, in the shell, scrubbed
12 clams, in the shell, scrubbed
1 tablespoon extra-virgin olive oil
4 cloves garlic, thinly sliced
One 28-ounce can crushed tomatoes
¹/₄ cup sherry
¹/₄ cup chopped fresh basil
1 ¹/₂ teaspoons dried oregano, crushed

$^{1}/_{4}$ teaspoon salt

$^{1}/_{4}$ teaspoon freshly ground black pepper

$^{1}/_{8}$ teaspoon red-pepper flakes

$^{3}/_{4}$ pound calamari (squid), cleaned, tentacles sliced, bodies sliced into rings

8 raw medium-size shrimp, peeled and deveined

12 ounces pasta (your favorite shape), cooked al dente

1. Combine the wine, water, and $^{1}/_{4}$ cup of the onion in a large pot. Bring to a boil, reduce the heat to low, and simmer for 5 minutes. Add the mussels and clams, cover tightly, and steam until all the shellfish have opened, about 3 minutes. Remove from the heat and set aside.

2. Heat the olive oil and garlic in a large pot or skillet until the garlic sizzles. Add the remaining onion and cook, covered, over low heat until the onion is soft and translucent, about 15 minutes. Add the tomatoes, sherry, basil, oregano, salt, pepper, and red-pepper flakes and simmer, uncovered, for 10 minutes.

3. Add the calamari to the tomato mixture and cook for 2 minutes. Add the shrimp and the cooked mussels and clams plus their cooking liquid. Mix well and continue to cook until the shrimp turn pink and opaque, 2 minutes more; do not overcook. Serve immediately over the pasta.

Makes 6 servings

Each serving contains approximately

Calories: 380

Fat: 5 g

Cholesterol: 143 mg

Sodium: 506 mg

Scampi-Style Shrimp with Spaghetti and Zucchini

᧰

Scampi is actually the Italian word for the tail portion of any of several varieties of lobsterettes, the best known being the prawn or shrimp. However, on American restaurant menus the term is often used to describe large shrimp that are split and cooked in garlic oil or butter.

This scampi dish is a revision of a reader's recipe that called for 6 tablespoons of butter or margarine and 2 tablespoons of olive oil. I was able to achieve the same taste and almost the same texture with considerably less of both.

I like to serve my version over a combination of spaghetti and zucchini squash, but you can toss it all together if you prefer.

1 pound raw medium-size shrimp, shelled and deveined (2 cups)
2 tablespoons corn-oil margarine

1 tablespoon finely chopped green onion (scallion), including green top
½ tablespoon extra-virgin olive oil
5 cloves garlic, pressed or minced
1 tablespoon fresh lemon juice
¼ teaspoon salt
2 tablespoons finely chopped fresh parsley
¼ teaspoon grated lemon zest
Dash of Tabasco
8 ounces zucchini squash, shredded (2 cups)
8 ounces spaghetti, cooked al dente
Lemon slices or wedges, for garnish (optional)

1. After cleaning the shrimp, pat them dry with paper towels and set aside.

2. Melt the margarine in a large skillet over medium heat. Stir in the green onion, olive oil, garlic, lemon juice, and salt, and cook until bubbly. Add the shrimp and cook, stirring constantly, until the shrimp turn from translucent to opaque and are pink in color, about 2 minutes. Stir in the parsley, lemon zest, and Tabasco. Remove the shrimp with a slotted spoon to a bowl. Add the zucchini and stir-fry over medium-high heat until tender, about 2 minutes.

3. To serve, spoon 1 cup of the cooked spaghetti onto each of 4 plates. Top with ½ cup of the zucchini and ½ cup of the shrimp. Serve immediately.

Makes 4 servings

Each serving contains approximately
Calories: 488
Fat: 11 g
Cholesterol: 173 mg
Sodium: 389 mg

Pasta with Clam Sauce

᧒

I designed this hearty, Italian pasta dish with one eye on the budget and the other on the clock, and it has become a family favorite.

One 6 ¹/₂-ounce can chopped clams
1 tablespoon extra-virgin olive oil
2 cloves garlic, pressed or minced
1 teaspoon anchovy paste
2 tablespoons finely chopped parsley
One 14 ¹/₂-ounce can chopped tomatoes, undrained
¹/₈ teaspoon freshly ground black pepper
1 teaspoon fresh lemon juice
6 ounces pasta, cooked al dente
2 sprigs Italian parsley, for garnish (optional)

1. Drain the clams, reserving the juice. Cover the clams and set aside.

2. Heat the olive oil in a medium-size skillet over medium heat. Add the garlic and cook just until it starts to sizzle. Stir in the anchovy paste, mixing well. Add the chopped parsley, the tomatoes, plus all the juice from the can, and the pepper. Mix them well and slowly bring the mixture to a boil. Reduce the heat to low and simmer,

uncovered, for 15 minutes. Remove from the heat and stir in the reserved clams and lemon juice.

3. To serve, place 1 ½ cups of cooked pasta on each of two plates. Top each serving with a cup of the clam sauce, or toss the sauce with the pasta if you prefer. Garnish with the sprigs of parsley if desired.

Makes 2 servings

Each serving contains approximately
Calories: 410
Fat: 9 g
Cholesterol: 48 mg
Sodium: 634 mg

Pasta Fisherman

⟋

For a change, substitute pasta shells for the spaghetti in
this dish. Also, mix the pasta into the sauce before
serving if you prefer.

---

2 teaspoons extra-virgin olive oil
1 clove garlic, minced
1 small onion, chopped (1 cup)
$\frac{1}{2}$ pound white mushrooms, chopped (2 $\frac{1}{2}$ cups)
2 tablespoons dry white wine
Three 8-ounce cans tomato sauce
$\frac{1}{3}$ cup nonfat cream cheese
Dash each salt and pepper, or to taste
$\frac{1}{2}$ pound crab meat, cut up
$\frac{1}{2}$ pound raw medium-size shrimp, peeled and deveined
1 pound spaghetti, cooked al dente
$\frac{1}{4}$ cup freshly grated Parmesan cheese

1. In a large, nonstick skillet, heat the oil over medium-high heat.
Add the garlic and cook until golden, 3 to 4 minutes. Add the onion,
mushrooms, and wine and simmer for 3 minutes. Add the tomato
sauce, cream cheese, salt, and pepper, and heat, stirring, until the
sauce begins to simmer.

2. Add the crab and shrimp to the sauce mixture; stir and simmer until the shrimp turns from translucent to opaque, about 3 minutes more. If using precooked seafood, simply heat through. Do not over-cook.

3. To serve, pour the sauce over the cooked spaghetti and sprinkle with the Parmesan cheese.

Makes 6 servings

Each serving contains approximately
Calories: 446
Fat: 5 g
Cholesterol: 78 mg
Sodium: 1,234 mg

Asian Pasta with Bay Scallops

ᘐ

This deliciously different, East-meets-West pasta dish was created by my stepson, Mark Breitenberg, for a small dinner party. I told him that I was not leaving his house without the recipe because it would be perfect for my column. If you can't find bay scallops, substitute shrimp or even cubed firm fish fillets. You can also use plain dry pasta in place of fresh, but the color of the red pepper pasta is sensational in this dish.

Sauce

2 tablespoons peeled and grated fresh ginger
2 cloves garlic, pressed or minced
1 tablespoon reduced-sodium soy sauce
1 tablespoon oyster sauce
1 tablespoon rice wine vinegar
2 tablespoons Chinese rice wine or sherry
2 tablespoons dark sesame oil
2 tablespoon fresh lime juice
1 tablespoon sugar

1 bunch green onions (scallions)
¹/₂ cup fat-free chicken stock
1 pound bay scallops
¹/₂ cup chopped fresh cilantro
12 ounces fresh red pepper pasta, cooked al dente
4 cilantro sprigs, for garnish (optional)

1. Combine all the sauce ingredients and set aside.

2. Finely chop the white parts of the green onions. Set the green tops aside. Combine the white parts of the green onions and the stock in a large skillet, set over medium heat, and cook the green onions until they are soft, about 3 minutes. Add the sauce ingredients to the skillet and mix well. Add the scallops and cook until they turn from translucent to opaque, 2 to 3 minutes. Do not overcook. Remove the skillet from the heat and stir in the cilantro and the green onion tops.

3. Pour the scallop mixture over the cooked pasta and mix well. Divide it equally among four plates. Garnish with the cilantro sprigs if desired.

Makes 4 servings

Each serving contains approximately
Calories: 464
Fat: 12 g
Cholesterol: 143 mg
Sodium: 378 mg

Old-Fashioned Tuna–Olive Macaroni Loaf

✌

I call this dish "old-fashioned" because the original recipe sent to me by a reader for revision was on the yellowed and slightly torn page she had cut out of a magazine forty years ago. Amazingly enough, even back then, the recipe was touting fewer calories because it was made with canned evaporated milk rather than cream.

Even with all my changes, which greatly reduce the amount of fat and cholesterol in each serving, this is still a very tasty dish to prepare. The trick is to choose an aged cheese which gives more flavor. This loaf can be made ahead of time and it is equally good served hot or cold.

8 ounces elbow macaroni
2 tablespoons corn-oil margarine
2 large eggs
2 large egg whites
2 tablespoons grated onion

Two 6-ounce cans water-packed white tuna, drained and flaked
12 pimiento-stuffed green olives, thinly sliced (¼ cup)
1 cup soft whole-wheat bread crumbs (2 slices bread)
One 12-ounce can evaporated skim milk
½ teaspoon salt
1 teaspoon dry mustard
1 tablespoon prepared horseradish
8 ounces reduced-fat sharp Cheddar cheese, grated

1. Preheat the oven to 350° F. Line a standard-size loaf pan with aluminum foil. Spray the foil-lined pan with nonstick vegetable spray and set it aside.

2. Cook the macaroni in a large pot of boiling water until al dente. Drain it thoroughly and add the margarine, stirring until it melts. Set it aside.

3. Combine the eggs and egg whites in a large bowl and beat them lightly. Add the onion, tuna, olives, and bread crumbs and mix well.

4. In a large saucepan combine the milk, salt, dry mustard, and horseradish. Mix well and bring to a boil over medium heat. Reduce the heat to low and simmer for 2 minutes. Add the cheese and stir just until it starts to melt, then pour it into the tuna mixture in the bowl. Add the macaroni and mix well. Carefully spoon the mixture into the prepared pan and using your hands, press it down firmly.

5. Bake in the preheated oven until a golden brown, about 1 hour. Allow to cool for 10 minutes before turning it over onto a serving dish or cutting board and cutting it into 8 slices.

Makes 8 servings

Each serving contains approximately
Calories: 356
Fat: 13 g
Cholesterol: 87 mg
Sodium: 715 mg

Clam and Mushroom Lasagna

ஃ

This rather nontraditional lasagna is a nice change from the more usual meat and red sauce versions. It also offers a delightful surprise for your guests at dinner parties.

1 medium-size onion, finely chopped (1 ¹/₂ cups)
2 cloves garlic, pressed or minced
1 pound white mushrooms, sliced (4 cups)
Three 6 ¹/₂-ounce cans chopped clams, undrained
One 12-ounce can evaporated skim milk
2 tablespoons corn-oil margarine
3 tablespoons all-purpose flour
¹/₄ teaspoon freshly ground black pepper
³/₄ teaspoon dried oregano, crushed
1 ¹/₂ teaspoons dried thyme, crushed
¹/₂ cup finely chopped fresh parsley
¹/₂ pound lasagna noodles, cooked al dente
One 15-ounce carton fat-free ricotta cheese
8 ounces shredded, part-skim mozzarella cheese
¹/₂ cup fresh, whole-wheat bread crumbs (1 slice ground)

1. Preheat the oven to 350° F.

2. Combine the onion and garlic in a large, nonstick skillet and cook over medium-low heat until the onion is translucent. Add a little water if necessary to prevent scorching. Add the mushrooms and cook them until soft, about 5 minutes. Set aside.

3. Drain the clams, reserving the liquid. Set the clams aside. Combine the clam juice and the milk and heat until bubbles appear around the edge either in a microwave oven or on the top of the stove. Melt the margarine in a 2- or 3-quart saucepan over medium-low heat. Add the flour and cook, stirring constantly for 2 minutes. Add the hot clam juice and milk mixture all at once, stirring constantly with a wire whisk. Bring to a boil over medium-low heat, reduce the heat to low and simmer, stirring frequently, until the mixture starts to thicken, about 5 minutes. Remove the saucepan from the heat and add the pepper, oregano, and thyme and mix well. Stir in the reserved clams and the parsley and set aside.

4. Spray a 9 × 13-inch baking dish with nonstick vegetable spray. Spread one-half of the mushroom mixture evenly over the bottom of the dish. Cover with a layer of the cooked lasagna noodles. Top the noodles with all the ricotta cheese and one-third of the clams. Add a second layer of noodles. Spread the remaining mushroom mixture over the noodles. Cover with half of the remaining clams. Sprinkle half of the mozzarella cheese evenly over the top. Top with the remaining noodles, clams, and mozzarella cheese. Sprinkle the bread crumbs evenly over the top.

5. Bake, uncovered, in the preheated oven until bubbling and lightly browned, about 30 minutes. Allow to stand for 5 minutes before cutting into eight approximately 3 × 4-inch servings.

Makes 8 servings

Each serving contains approximately
Calories: 353
Fat: 9 g
Cholesterol: 46 mg
Sodium: 663 mg

Pasta with Lemon Chicken

∂

This is a revision of a reader's recipe that called for canned mushrooms. In this recipe I have used fresh wild mushrooms. Even though it does take a little longer to cook them, they greatly improve the taste of the dish.

1 tablespoon extra-virgin olive oil
2 cloves garlic, pressed or minced
1 pound boneless, skinless chicken breasts, cut lengthwise into
    $^1\!/_2$-inch strips
$^1\!/_2$ pound fresh wild mushrooms, sliced (2 cups)
1 tablespoon fresh lemon juice
1 teaspoon butter-flavored sprinkles
$^1\!/_2$ teaspoon dried oregano, crushed
$^1\!/_4$ teaspoon freshly ground black pepper
1 $^1\!/_2$ cups fat-free chicken stock
2 tablespoons cornstarch
1 pound pasta, cooked al dente
2 tablespoons finely chopped fresh parsley

1. In a large, nonstick skillet, heat the olive oil over medium heat. Add the garlic and cook just until it sizzles. Add the chicken and cook, stirring, until it is no longer pink, about 4 minutes. Remove the chicken from the skillet and set aside.

2. In the same skillet over medium heat, place the mushrooms and cook and stir until lightly browned, 5 minutes. Add the lemon juice, butter-flavored sprinkles, oregano, and pepper.

3. In a separate bowl, combine the stock and cornstarch, stirring until the cornstarch is completely dissolved. Add this to the mushroom mixture along with the chicken and simmer, stirring constantly, over medium heat until the sauce thickens, about 3 minutes. Serve over the hot pasta, or toss with the pasta, and sprinkle with the parsley.

Makes 4 servings

Each serving contains approximately
Calories: 634
Fat: 9 g
Cholesterol: 72 mg
Sodium: 99 mg

Angel-Hair Pasta with Herbed Chicken

✥

If you don't have any chicken, you can substitute two 6-ounce cans or one 12-ounce can of drained, water-packed white tuna in this recipe.

1 teaspoon extra-virgin olive oil
2 tablespoons finely chopped onion
1 carrot, cut into small dice (^{1}/$_2$ cup)
3 boneless, skinless chicken breast halves (12 ounces), cut into
 ^{1}/$_2$-inch dice
^{1}/$_2$ teaspoon dried basil, crushed
^{1}/$_2$ teaspoon dried oregano, crushed
^{1}/$_8$ teaspoon dried thyme, crushed
^{1}/$_8$ teaspoon freshly ground black pepper
1 ^{1}/$_2$ cups small broccoli florets
One 12-ounce can evaporated skim milk
9 ounces fresh angel-hair pasta
^{3}/$_4$ cup freshly grated Parmesan cheese

1. Heat the olive oil in a large, nonstick skillet. Add the onion and carrot and cook them, stirring, over medium heat until the onion is soft but not brown, about 5 minutes. Add some water if it seems dry.

2. Add the chicken to the skillet and cook, stirring, just until it is no longer pink, about 4 minutes. Sprinkle with the basil, oregano, thyme, and pepper. Add the broccoli, cover, and steam for 5 minutes. Stir in the milk and warm it, but do not allow it to boil.

3. Meanwhile, cook the pasta in a large pot of boiling water until al dente; drain well. Stir the pasta into the sauce mixture, then add the cheese. Cover the pan until the sauce has thickened slightly, 3 to 5 minutes. Serve immediately.

Makes four 1 ³/₄-cup servings

Each serving contains approximately
Calories: 461
Fat: 8 g
Cholesterol: 64 mg
Sodium: 455 mg

Chicken Sorrento

❧

This is a revision of a very high-fat dish sent to me by a reader in Milwaukee. She wrote and told me how much her family enjoyed my lighter version of the dish and how much better she felt about making it for them.

3 tablespoons all-purpose flour
1 teaspoon dried parsley flakes
1 teaspoon salt
$^1/_8$ teaspoon freshly ground black pepper
6 boneless, skinless chicken breast halves
1 tablespoon corn-oil margarine
One 4-ounce can sliced mushrooms, drained
One 10 $^3/_4$-ounce can low-fat cream of celery soup
1 teaspoon dried oregano, crushed
One 16-ounce container nonfat sour cream
4 ounces macaroni, cooked al dente
One 10-ounce package frozen peas, thawed
Paprika, for garnish

1. Preheat the oven to 350° F. Spray a 7 × 11-inch baking dish with nonstick vegetable spray and set aside.

2. In a plastic bag, combine the flour, parsley flakes, salt, and pepper. Add the chicken breasts, one at a time, and coat with the flour mixture.

3. Melt the margarine in a large, nonstick skillet over medium heat. Add the chicken and cook until golden brown, about 5 minutes on each side. Remove the chicken from the pan and set aside.

4. Add the mushrooms to the skillet and cook, stirring frequently, over low heat, until they are tender, about 5 minutes. Stir in the soup and oregano. Remove the skillet from the heat and stir in the sour cream.

5. Place the cooked macaroni in the bottom of the prepared baking dish. Stir in half of the soup mixture and all the peas. Arrange the chicken over the top and spoon the remaining soup mixture over the chicken. Sprinkle with paprika and bake, covered, for 40 minutes. Uncover and bake until bubbly, an additional 20 minutes.

Makes 6 servings

Each serving contains approximately
Calories: 400
Fat: 8 g
Cholesterol: 88 mg
Sodium: 858 mg

Chicken Lasagna

⁊

This is a great company dish because it can be made ahead of time and baked just before you plan to serve it.

---

2 tablespoons corn-oil margarine
6 tablespoons unbleached all-purpose flour
1 ½ cups fat-free chicken stock, hot
1 cup nonfat milk, hot
1 large clove garlic, pressed or minced
½ teaspoon salt (omit if using salted stock)
¼ teaspoon freshly ground black pepper
One 4-ounce can sliced mushrooms
½ cup nonfat sour cream
½ cup nonfat sandwich spread, such as Miracle Whip
8 lasagna noodles, cooked al dente
3 cups chopped cooked chicken
8 ounces reduced-fat sharp Cheddar cheese, grated (2 cups)

1. Preheat the oven to 350° F. Spray a 9 × 13-inch baking dish with nonstick vegetable spray.

2. Melt the margarine in a medium-size saucepan. Add the flour and stir over medium heat for 2 minutes. Do not brown. Add the hot stock and milk and stir over medium heat, using a wire whisk, until

the mixture comes to a boil. Add the garlic, salt, pepper, and mush-rooms, and continue to cook for 1 minute more. Remove from the heat and stir in the sour cream and sandwich spread.

3. Layer half the noodles, half the chicken, half the sauce, and half the cheese in the prepared dish. Repeat the layers and bake until bubbly, 30 minutes. Let it rest for 5 minutes before serving.

Makes 8 servings

Each serving contains approximately
Calories: 375
Fat: 15 g
Cholesterol: 68 mg
Sodium: 552 mg

Smoked Turkey Pasta with Dried-Tomato Sauce

ও

The "secret" ingredient that makes this hearty pasta dish so delicious and satisfying is the dried tomato. Its intense flavor, deep color, and slightly chewy texture add enormously to the taste of almost any dish.

One 10 ¾-ounce can low-fat cream of chicken soup
⅔ cup dried Sonoma tomato bits
¼ teaspoon freshly ground black pepper
2 cloves garlic, pressed or minced; or ¼ teaspoon garlic powder
1 ½ teaspoons Italian herb blend, crushed
One 10-ounce package frozen peas, thawed (2 cups)
8 ounces boneless, skinless smoked turkey breast, diced (2 cups)
8 ounces rotini pasta, cooked al dente
½ cup freshly grated Parmesan cheese (optional)

1. Combine the soup and one soup can of either water or skim milk in a large saucepan. Add the dried tomatoes, pepper, garlic, and Italian herbs and bring to a boil over medium heat. Reduce heat to low and simmer, stirring frequently, for 5 minutes.

2. Stir in the peas and smoked turkey and heat the mixture through.

3. Remove the saucepan from the heat and stir in the cooked pasta.

Makes four 2-cup servings

Each serving contains approximately
Calories: 425
Fat: 5 g
Cholesterol: 31 mg
Sodium: 932 mg

Dried Tomatoes

The Italians were the first to dry tomatoes by hanging or laying them out in the sun as a practical way to preserve their abundant summer crop for consumption during the winter months. In fact, until recently all the dried tomatoes available in this country were imported from Italy. Sun drying is now obsolete because the tomatoes have to be treated with sulphur dioxide to keep the bugs away, which destroys much of their flavor. Today, tomatoes are dried in large dehydrators to avoid the hazards of weather, bugs, or debris and to ensure a pure tomato flavor.

The first American-grown dried tomatoes were introduced by Ruth Waltenspiel in the Sonoma Valley region of California. She already was in the business of drying fruit and started drying tomatoes as a favor for her Italian-American neighbors. As more and more well-known chefs started using dried tomatoes in recipes, the demand for them grew, and Ruth started to sell her dried tomatoes all over the country. Dried tomatoes are available in halves, bits, or marinated in olive oil.

Turkey Lasagna with Cranberry Sauce

~

This is a wonderful one-dish meal for all of your holiday entertaining and is sure to be a conversation piece. It also makes a nontraditional entree for a Thanksgiving dinner, and it's perfect for using up turkey leftovers after the holiday. Any way it's served, this truly unusual pasta dish is sure to get rave reviews from your family and friends.

1 ½ cups fat-free chicken stock
One 12-ounce can evaporated skim milk
2 tablespoons corn-oil margarine
3 tablespoons all-purpose flour
¼ teaspoon salt (omit if using salted stock)
¼ teaspoon freshly ground black pepper
¾ teaspoon dried sage, crushed
1 ½ teaspoons dried thyme, crushed
3 cups chopped or ground cooked turkey
½ cup finely chopped fresh parsley
One 16-ounce can whole berry cranberry sauce
½ pound lasagna noodles, cooked al dente

One 15-ounce carton fat-free ricotta cheese
8 ounces part-skim mozzarella cheese, shredded
½ cup fresh whole-wheat bread crumbs (1 slice ground)

1. Preheat the oven to 350° F. Spray a 9 × 13-inch shallow baking dish with nonstick vegetable spray.

2. Combine the stock and milk and heat until bubbles appear around the edge either in a microwave oven or on the top of the stove.

3. Melt the margarine in a 2- or 3-quart saucepan over medium-low heat. Add the flour and cook, stirring constantly, for 2 minutes. Add the hot stock and milk mixture all at once, stirring constantly with a wire whisk. Bring to a boil, reduce the heat to low and simmer, stirring frequently, until the mixture starts to thicken, about 5 minutes. Remove from the heat and add the salt, pepper, sage, and thyme and mix well. Stir in the turkey and parsley and set aside.

4. Spread half of the cranberry sauce evenly over the bottom of the prepared dish. Cover the sauce with a layer of the cooked lasagna noodles. Top the noodles with all the ricotta cheese and one-third of the turkey mixture. Add a second layer of noodles. Spread the remaining cranberry sauce over the noodles. Cover the cranberries with half of the remaining turkey mixture. Sprinkle half of the mozzarella cheese evenly over the top. Top with the remaining noodles, turkey mixture, and mozzarella cheese. Sprinkle the bread crumbs evenly over the top.

5. Bake, uncovered, in the preheated oven until bubbling and lightly browned, 30 minutes. Allow to stand for 5 minutes before cutting into eight approximately 3 × 4-inch servings.

Makes 8 servings

Each serving contains approximately
Calories: 472
Fat: 10 g
Cholesterol: 61 mg
Sodium: 406 mg

Beef and Broccoli Pasta with Dried-Tomato Sauce

ॐ

This hearty meal is sure to be a favorite with the whole family. If you have any of this dish left over, serve it cold as a pasta salad.

---

1 $\frac{1}{2}$ cups fat-free beef stock
One 12-ounce can evaporated skim milk
2 tablespoons corn-oil margarine
3 tablespoons unbleached all-purpose flour
$\frac{1}{2}$ cup dried tomato halves, cut into strips
$\frac{1}{4}$ teaspoon salt (omit if using salted stock)
$\frac{1}{4}$ teaspoon freshly ground black pepper
$\frac{1}{4}$ teaspoon dried rosemary, crushed
$\frac{3}{4}$ teaspoon dried oregano, crushed
1 teaspoon dried thyme, crushed
1 pound lean ground round
2 cups broccoli florets, steamed crisp-tender
8 ounces rotini pasta, cooked al dente
6 tablespoons freshly grated Parmesan cheese

1. Combine the stock and milk and bring to boiling point, either in a microwave oven or on top of the stove.

2. Meanwhile, melt the margarine in a 2- or 3-quart saucepan over medium heat. Add the flour and cook, stirring constantly, for 2 minutes. Add the hot stock and milk mixture, all at once, stirring constantly with a wire whisk. Bring to a boil and reduce the heat to low. Add the dried tomatoes, salt, pepper, rosemary, oregano, and thyme and cook, stirring frequently, for 5 minutes.

3. While the sauce is cooking, put the ground meat in a medium-size, nonstick skillet and cook over medium heat, stirring frequently, until it loses its red color and crumbles, about 5 minutes.

4. Add the cooked meat and the broccoli to the sauce and heat through. Remove from the heat and stir in the cooked pasta. Top each serving with 1 tablespoon of the Parmesan cheese.

Makes 6 servings

Each serving contains approximately
Calories: 456
Fat: 17 g
Cholesterol: 64 mg
Sodium: 429 mg

Lemon-Scented Steak on Soba Noodles

ᲔᲠ

In this recipe I suggest marinating the steak for at least one hour before cooking it. It's even better, however, if it marinates all day. Also, you can substitute orange juice and orange zest for the lemon called for in this recipe if you prefer.

1 pound flank or lean round steak, all visible fat removed

Marinade
2 tablespoons reduced-sodium soy sauce
3 tablespoons Chinese rice wine or sherry
1 tablespoon peanut oil
2 teaspoons sugar
1/4 cup fresh lemon juice

1 teaspoon cornstarch
1 teaspoon reduced-sodium soy sauce
2 teaspoons rice vinegar
2 teaspoons sugar

1 bunch green onions (scallions), sliced diagonally into 1-inch pieces
    (1 ½ cups)
1 large red bell pepper, thinly sliced (2 cups)
1 tablespoon fresh ginger, peeled and minced
2 tablespoons grated lemon zest
8 ounces soba noodles, cooked al dente

1. Cut the flank steak into strips about ¼ inch wide.

2. Combine all the marinade ingredients in a large bowl and mix well. Stir in the sliced steak, cover tightly, and refrigerate for at least 1 hour.

3. In another bowl, combine the cornstarch, soy sauce, vinegar, and sugar. Mix well, and set aside.

4. Heat 1 tablespoon of the marinade in a large skillet or wok over high heat. Add the beef, green onions, bell pepper, ginger, and lemon zest and stir-fry just until the beef loses its red color, about 1 minute. Spoon the beef and vegetable mixture into a bowl. Add the remaining marinade to the skillet and return to high heat. Stir in the cornstarch mixture and cook just until it thickens slightly. Return the beef and vegetables to the skillet and stir-fry just long enough to mix well.

5. To serve, spoon one-quarter of the mixture over 1 cup of the soba noodles for each serving. Or toss everything together before serving.

Makes 4 servings

Each serving contains approximately
Calories: 398
Fat: 16 g
Cholesterol: 61 mg
Sodium: 416 mg

Beef and Pasta Provençal

ᘒ

Fennel is one of my favorite vegetables. This aromatic plant tastes like a very mild licorice or anise. Yet it is sweeter and more delicate than either one. It has a broad bulbous base and celerylike stems that are treated like a vegetable. The feathery, fernlike foliage resembles fresh dill and is used as an herb. It also makes a beautiful plate garnish.

If you have pots big enough to hold larger amounts of this dish, it is a great one-dish meal for parties. When increasing the volume, however, be careful not to use too much cayenne pepper. If you double or triple the amount called for, the dish will be too hot for most people's tastes. I suggest using only the amount called for in this recipe and then adding more of it to taste at the end.

---

1 tablespoon olive oil
3 cloves garlic, pressed or minced
1 pound very lean ground beef
1 large onion, chopped (2 cups)
1 large or 2 small bulbs fennel (1 ½ pounds total), including
  fern, chopped (4 cups)

One 14 ½-ounce can ready-cut tomatoes, undrained
2 teaspoons dried thyme, crushed
2 bay leaves
½ teaspoon salt (omit if using salted stock)
½ teaspoon freshly ground black pepper
¼ teaspoon cayenne pepper, or to taste
¼ cup Pernod or other anise-flavored alcohol
8 ounces whole-wheat pasta
1 cup fat-free chicken stock
¾ cup freshly grated Parmesan cheese
Fresh thyme sprigs, for garnish (optional)

1. Heat the olive oil and garlic in a large saucepan or a Dutch oven until the garlic sizzles. Add the ground beef and cook, stirring frequently, over medium-high heat until it is crumbled and no longer red. Add the onion and continue to cook over medium heat until the onion is soft and translucent. Add the fennel, tomatoes, thyme, bay leaves, salt, pepper, and cayenne and mix well and slowly bring to a boil. Reduce heat to low and simmer for 30 minutes. Add the Pernod and cook for another 10 minutes.

2. While the meat and vegetables are cooking, cook the pasta in a large pot of boiling water until tender but still very firm. Drain thoroughly and return to the pot. Add the stock to the pasta and simmer until most of the stock has been absorbed, 2 to 3 minutes. Add the pasta to the meat mixture and mix well. Garnish each serving with 2 tablespoons of the Parmesan cheese and, if desired, the sprigs of fresh thyme.

Makes six 1 ¾-cup servings

Each serving contains approximately
Calories: 355
Fat: 12 g
Cholesterol: 102 mg
Sodium: 624 mg

Penne with Spicy Sausage and Broccoli

ॐ

This is one of those hearty, soul-satisfying dishes that is easy to make in large quantities and perfect for a hungry crowd after a football game on a chilly fall night.

½ pound low-fat spicy sausage, any casing discarded
¼ cup plus 2 tablespoons water
1 tablespoon extra-virgin olive oil
2 cloves garlic, pressed or minced
1 pound broccoli florets, steamed crisp-tender
1 pound penne pasta, cooked al dente
⅓ cup freshly grated Romano cheese

1. Combine the sausage and ¼ cup of the water in a large skillet and cook over medium-high heat, breaking the sausage up with the back of a spoon as it cooks. Allow the water to evaporate and brown the sausage.

2. Add the 2 remaining tablespoons of water and stir to loosen the browned bits of sausage from the bottom of the pan. Add the olive

oil and garlic and cook just until the garlic starts to sizzle. Add the broccoli and cook until heated through.

3. Stir in the cooked pasta and cheese and serve immediately.

Makes 8 servings

Each serving contains approximately
Calories: 302
Fat: 7 g
Cholesterol: 19 mg
Sodium: 252 mg

Grains
and
Beans

Curried Lentils and Rice

ॐ

This recipe is adapted from one in the book, *Beyond Alfalfa Sprouts and Cheese,* by Joy Kirkpatrick and Judy Gillard. I reviewed their book in my column, and this version of the recipe has become one of my favorite tailgate party dishes. It is tasty, easy to make, and very inexpensive.

---

2 cloves garlic, minced
1 small onion, chopped
2 tablespoons peeled and minced fresh ginger
$\frac{1}{2}$ teaspoon ground turmeric
$\frac{1}{2}$ teaspoon cumin seeds, crushed; or $\frac{1}{4}$ teaspoon ground cumin
$\frac{1}{4}$ teaspoon ground allspice
2 teaspoons curry powder
1 cup brown, green, or even pink lentils, washed
$\frac{3}{4}$ cup raw brown rice, washed
3 cups water

1. Spray a large, heavy saucepan with nonstick vegetable spray. Set the pan over medium heat. Add the garlic, onion, and ginger and cook until golden brown, about 4 minutes. Add the turmeric, cumin, allspice, and curry and cook for 2 more minutes.

2. Add the lentils and rice and mix well. Stir in the water and bring to a boil over high heat. Reduce the heat to low and cook, covered, until the lentils and rice are tender and all the liquid is absorbed, 35 to 45 minutes. If necessary, add a few more tablespoons of the water to cook until the rice is tender.

3. Remove from the heat and allow to stand, covered, for 10 minutes before serving.

Makes six 1-cup servings

Each serving contains approximately
Calories: 73
Fat: Negligible
Cholesterol: None
Sodium: 71 mg

Oat Groat Pilaf with Beans and Cheese

ॐ

Oat groats offer a delightful change from the more usual rice. You can substitute other vegetables for the green beans in this recipe and also add other types of cheese.

This recipe can easily be reheated. Add 2 to 3 tablespoons of vegetable stock to the cold oat groat mixture and mix thoroughly. Cover and bake in a preheated 300° F oven until heated through, about 25 minutes.

---

1 ¹/₂ *teaspoons corn oil*
1 *cup oat groats*
¹/₂ *medium-size onion, thinly sliced (1 cup)*
1 ¹/₄ *cups vegetable stock*
1 *tablespoon reduced-sodium soy sauce*
1 *teaspoon dried thyme, crushed*
4 *cups French-cut green beans*
1 *cup grated, fat-reduced Swiss cheese*

1. Heat the oil in a large, heavy skillet. Add the oat groats and the onion and cook them, stirring frequently, over medium heat until brown. Add the stock, soy sauce, and thyme and bring to a boil. Reduce the heat to low and cook, covered, until the liquid is absorbed, about 1 hour.

2. Stir in the beans and sprinkle the grated cheese over the top. Cover and cook until the cheese has melted.

Makes four 1 ½-cup servings

Each serving contains approximately
Calories: 200
Fat: 5 g
Cholesterol: None
Sodium: 125 mg

Soft Fontina Polenta with Wild Mushrooms

⤳

A few years ago The International Food and Lifestyle Media Conference was held in Chicago. One night during the conference the dinner was a giant buffet called "A Taste of the Windy City." At this event twenty-five of Chicago's leading restaurants each served one of its most popular dishes for the guests to taste. This delightful Italian dish was offered by the Bella Vista Restaurant.

Because it was one of my favorites, I asked for the recipe to share with my readers. At the Bella Vista Restaurant they serve their polenta with a little white truffle oil drizzled over the top. I omitted this step from my recipe due to both cost and lack of availability.

4 cups water
¹/₂ teaspoon salt
1 cup yellow cornmeal
1 tablespoon extra-virgin olive oil
2 cloves garlic, thinly sliced

½ pound fresh wild mushrooms such as shiitake, crimini, portabella,
    or porcini, thinly sliced
2 cups fat-free chicken stock
¼ teaspoon salt (omit if using salted stock)
¼ teaspoon freshly ground black pepper
1 teaspoon dried thyme, crushed
½ teaspoon dried rosemary, crushed
¼ cup finely chopped fresh parsley
3 ounces Fontina cheese, diced
¼ cup nonfat milk
¼ cup freshly grated Parmesan cheese

1. Combine the water and salt in a saucepan that has a tight-fitting lid and bring to a boil over medium heat. Add the cornmeal in a steady stream, stirring constantly. Continue to stir until the mixture starts to thicken, about 2 minutes. Reduce the heat to low and cook, covered, for 1 hour, stirring every 15 minutes.

2. Heat the oil in a large, nonstick skillet over medium heat. Add the garlic and cook until lightly toasted, 2 to 3 minutes. Add the mushrooms and cook, stirring frequently, until tender, about 5 minutes. Add the stock, salt, pepper, thyme, and rosemary and cook until the liquid is reduced by half, about 10 minutes. Stir in the parsley and set aside.

3. Remove the cooked polenta from the heat and stir in the Fontina cheese and milk. Continue stirring until the cheese is completely melted. Spoon 1 cup of the polenta into each of four bowls and top each serving with ½ cup of the sauce. Sprinkle 1 tablespoon of the Parmesan cheese over each one.

Makes 4 servings

Each serving contains approximately
Calories: 310
Fat: 14 g
Cholesterol: 30 mg
Sodium: 780 mg

Shrimp Conga

ॐ

This dish, named "conga" by the reader who sent it, can be made with canned tuna as well as shrimp and any vegetable of your choice in place of the broccoli. Also, it is good served over pasta or on a baked potato as well as rice.

One 10-ounce package frozen chopped broccoli, thawed
1 pound raw medium-size shrimp, peeled and deveined
⅛ teaspoon salt
⅛ teaspoon freshly ground black pepper
3 tablespoons fresh lime juice
6 ounces nonfat cream cheese, at room temperature
1 ounce blue cheese, crumbled
2 teaspoons butter-flavored sprinkles
2 cups cooked rice

1. Preheat the oven to 400° F. Spray a 7 × 11-inch baking dish with nonstick vegetable spray.

2. Arrange the broccoli in a layer in the bottom of the dish. Place the shrimp on top of the broccoli and sprinkle with the salt, pepper, and lime juice. Combine the cheeses and butter-flavored sprinkles and spoon evenly over the shrimp.

3. Cover the dish with foil and bake until the shrimp turn from translucent to opaque, about 15 to 20 minutes for large shrimp and about 10 minutes for small ones. Remove from the oven and stir until it resembles a creamy broccoli sauce with shrimp.

4. To serve, spoon ¾ cup of the shrimp and broccoli mixture over ½ cup of the rice. Or stir the rice into the shrimp and broccoli mixture.

Makes 4 servings

Each serving contains approximately
Calories: 342
Fat: 5 g
Cholesterol: 185 mg
Sodium: 705 mg

Shrimp Creole

᪥

This quick and easy seafood favorite can also be made
with canned tuna in place of the shrimp.

1 medium-size onion, finely chopped (1 $^{1}/_{2}$ cups)
1 small green bell pepper, chopped (1 cup)
1 large rib celery, chopped ($^{1}/_{2}$ cup)
2 cloves garlic, pressed or minced
1 cup vegetable juice, such as V-8
One 16-ounce can chopped tomatoes, undrained
1 tablespoon fresh lemon juice
1 bay leaf
2 tablespoon chopped fresh parsley
1 teaspoon paprika
$^{1}/_{2}$ teaspoon salt
$^{1}/_{4}$ teaspoon cayenne pepper
1 tablespoon cornstarch
2 tablespoons water
1 pound medium-size shrimp, peeled and deveined
3 cups cooked rice

1. Combine the onion, bell pepper, celery, and garlic in a large skillet. Add the vegetable juice and cook over medium heat for 5 minutes. Add the tomatoes, lemon juice, bay leaf, parsley, paprika, salt, and cayenne pepper and mix well. Cover and simmer over low heat for 15 minutes.

2. Dissolve the cornstarch in the water and add it to the skillet. Stir until slightly thickened. Add the shrimp to the pan and continue to cook, covered, until the shrimp turns pink and opaque, about 3 more minutes.

3. To serve, place ³⁄₄ cup of the rice on each of four plates. Top each serving with 1 ¹⁄₂ cups of the shrimp mixture. Or if you prefer, combine the rice with the shrimp mixture before serving.

Makes 4 servings

Each serving contains approximately
Calories: 329
Fat: 3 g
Cholesterol: 173 mg
Sodium: 909 mg

Salmon Wiggle

◆

You can also chill this salmon mixture (without adding the rice) and use it as a spread for sandwiches or as a dip for chips.

---

1 tablespoon corn-oil margarine
3 tablespoons unbleached all-purpose flour
One 12-ounce can evaporated skim milk
One 14 ³/₄-ounce can red salmon, drained, liquid reserved
¹/₄ teaspoon salt
¹/₂ teaspoon freshly ground black pepper
2 large hard-boiled eggs, yolks discarded and whites chopped
1 cup frozen peas, thawed
2 cups cooked rice

1. Melt the margarine in a medium-size saucepan over medium heat. Add the flour and stir with a wire whisk for 1 minute, being careful not to let it brown. Slowly stir in the milk and reserved salmon liquid, salt, and pepper. Continue cooking, stirring constantly, until thickened, about 10 minutes.

2. Add the salmon, chopped egg whites, peas, and rice and cook until heated through, about 5 minutes more.

Makes four 1-cup servings

Each serving contains approximately
Calories: 423
Fat: 11 g
Cholesterol: 49 mg
Sodium: 882 mg

Chicken in Pink Peppercorn Sauce with Herbed Quinoa

ᔓ

This is both a delicious and unusual chicken dish. The sauce can either be served with the quinoa or mixed with it.

Quinoa (pronounced *keen-wah*) is a tiny, bead-shaped, ivory-colored grain with a bland flavor and a slightly chewy texture. It can be used like rice, but it's even quicker to cook. This ancient, South American grain is becoming increasingly popular in this country and is available in most supermarkets and all health food stores.

Herbed Quinoa
One 14 ½-ounce can fat-free chicken stock
¼ cup water
¼ teaspoon freshly ground black pepper
1 cup quinoa
1 tablespoon extra-virgin olive oil
1 teaspoon dried tarragon, crushed
¾ teaspoon dried thyme, crushed

Chicken

1 tablespoon corn-oil margarine
1 medium-size onion, chopped (1 ½ cups)
¼ cup brandy
2 tablespoons pink peppercorns
One 10 ¾-ounce can condensed low-fat cream of chicken soup
1 pound cooked boneless, skinless chicken breast halves, cut into strips
    (4 cups)
Fresh tarragon sprigs, for garnish (optional)

1. For the herbed quinoa, combine the stock, water, and pepper in a medium-size saucepan and bring to a boil over high heat. Stir in the quinoa, reduce the heat to low, and cook, covered, until all the liquid has been absorbed, about 12 minutes. Remove from the heat and stir in the olive oil, dried tarragon, and thyme. Cover again and allow to stand for 5 more minutes.

2. Meanwhile, prepare the chicken. Melt the margarine in a large skillet over low heat. Add the onion to the skillet and cook, stirring frequently, over low heat until soft and translucent, about 5 minutes. Turn the heat up to medium and continue cooking the onion until it starts to brown, about 5 minutes more. Add the brandy and peppercorns to the onion and cook until the liquid reduces by half. Add the soup, cooked chicken, and herbed quinoa and mix well. Bring back to a simmer over medium heat and immediately remove from the heat.

3. To serve, place 1 ⅓ cups of the mixture on each of six plates and garnish with the sprigs of tarragon if desired.

Makes 6 servings

Each serving contains approximately
Calories: 334
Fat: 9 g
Cholesterol: 70 mg
Sodium: 321 mg

Chinese Chicken and Rice

ॐ

All of the ingredients for this quick and easy recipe can be stored in the cupboard. It is a great dish to make when you're in a hurry and don't have time to go to the market.

---

¹/₄ cup slivered almonds
One 10 ³/₄-ounce can condensed low-fat cream of chicken soup
One 14 ¹/₂-ounce can fat-free chicken stock
1 tablespoon reduced-sodium soy sauce
1 teaspoon dark sesame oil
1 tablespoon dehydrated onion flakes
1 teaspoon Chinese five-spice blend
¹/₄ teaspoon garlic powder
One 8-ounce can sliced water chestnuts, drained
One 10-ounce can chunk white chicken, undrained
1 ¹/₂ cups raw instant rice
Sliced green onions (scallions), for garnish (optional)

1. Put the almonds in a skillet and cook them over medium heat until fragrant and well toasted, about 5 minutes. Set aside.

2. In a large saucepan, combine the soup, stock, soy sauce, sesame oil, onion flakes, spice blend, garlic powder, and water chestnuts and bring to a boil over medium-low heat. Reduce the heat to low and simmer for 5 minutes. Add the chicken and rice and mix well. Cover and remove from the heat. Allow to stand until all the liquid is absorbed, 5 minutes. Top each serving with 1 tablespoon of the toasted almonds. Garnish with the sliced green onions if desired.

Makes 4 servings

Each serving contains approximately
Calories: 369
Fat: 9 g
Cholesterol: 38 mg
Sodium: 622 mg

Sweet and Sour Turkey Balls with Brown Rice

⤳

I like to serve this tasty Asian dish in the middle of a large plate surrounded by stir-fried Chinese pea pods.

Turkey Balls

1 pound ground turkey
3 tablespoons reduced-sodium soy sauce
3 tablespoons Chinese rice wine or sherry
2 teaspoons peeled and minced fresh ginger
1 teaspoon sugar
2 cloves garlic, pressed or minced

Sauce

One 11-ounce can mandarin orange sections packed in juice
1 teaspoon cornstarch
1 tablespoon sugar
¼ cup rice vinegar
1 teaspoon reduced-sodium soy sauce
2 cups cooked brown rice

1. Combine all the turkey ball ingredients in a large bowl and mix well. Form the mixture into 12 balls.

2. Place the turkey balls on a steamer rack and cover with foil. Cook, covered, over simmering water, until cooked through, about 20 minutes.

3. While the turkey balls are cooking, make the sauce. Drain the mandarin oranges and pour the juice into a large saucepan. Set the orange sections aside. Add the cornstarch to the juice and stir until it has completely dissolved. Add all the remaining sauce ingredients, except the orange sections, and mix well. Cook over medium heat until the sauce is clear and thickened. Add the cooked turkey balls and orange sections to the sauce and mix well.

4. To serve, place 3 turkey balls on top of ½ cup of the rice for each serving. Spoon the sauce over the top of each serving. If you prefer, you can combine the rice with the sauce and turkey balls and serve it in a large bowl.

Makes 4 servings

Each serving contains approximately
Calories: 378
Fat: 14 g
Cholesterol: 86 mg
Sodium: 612 mg

Turkey à la Newburg on Herbed Wild Rice and Broccoli

ॐ

This dish was originally created using lobster by a chef at Delmonico's in New York many years ago for a regular customer named Wenburg. When the gentleman and the restaurant had a falling out, the chef renamed the dish "Newburg."

While the original recipe is far more complicated and expensive to make than this one, my simpler, more economical version is still an opulent-tasting dish.

---

2 ¼ cups fat-free chicken stock
¼ teaspoon salt (omit if using salted stock)
1 teaspoon dried thyme, crushed
¾ cup raw wild rice
2 tablespoons corn-oil margarine
3 tablespoons unbleached all-purpose flour
One 12-ounce can evaporated skim milk, warm
½ cup sherry

½ teaspoon paprika
⅛ teaspoon ground nutmeg
1 large egg, lightly beaten
3 cups diced cooked turkey meat (¾ pound)
2 cups broccoli florets, steamed crisp-tender

1. Combine the stock, salt, and thyme in a medium-size saucepan and bring to a boil over medium-high heat. Stir in the wild rice and cover. Cook over low heat until all the liquid is absorbed, 45 minutes.

2. While the wild rice is cooking, melt the margarine in another large saucepan. Add the flour and cook, stirring constantly, for 3 minutes. Add the warm milk and mix thoroughly. Stir in the sherry, paprika, and nutmeg and cook, stirring frequently, until thickened, about 5 minutes. Add a little of the hot sauce to the egg and mix well. Stir the egg mixture back into the sauce. Add the turkey and mix well. Remove from the heat.

3. To serve, combine the broccoli and wild rice and spoon 1 cup of the mixture onto each of four plates. Top each serving with 1 cup of the turkey mixture.

Makes four 2-cup servings

Each serving contains approximately
Calories: 478
Fat: 13 g
Cholesterol: 119 mg
Sodium: 688 mg

Curried Lamb and Rice

᧖

This dish is excellent for using up leftover lamb roast. You can also substitute cooked beef or pork for the lamb in the recipe. I like this curry even better the day after I make it because the flavors have a chance to "marry." I have also served it cold as a salad.

---

2 medium-size onions, finely chopped (3 cups)
2 teaspoons curry powder
1/2 teaspoon salt
1/8 teaspoon ground ginger
One 12-ounce can evaporated skim milk
1 tablespoon cornstarch
1/2 cup fat-free chicken stock
2 cups diced cooked lean lamb
One 14 1/2-ounce can ready-cut tomatoes, drained
1/4 cup mango chutney
2 cups cooked rice

1. In a large saucepan or soup kettle, cook the onions, covered, over very low heat for 30 minutes, adding a little water if necessary to prevent scorching. Stir in the curry powder, salt, ginger, and milk.

2. Dissolve the cornstarch in ¼ cup of the stock and add it to the onion mixture. Stir in the remaining stock and bring to a boil over medium heat. Reduce the heat to low and simmer until slightly thickened. Stir in the lamb, tomatoes, chutney, and rice and heat through.

Makes six 1 ¼-cup servings

Each serving contains approximately
Calories: 475
Fat: 7 g
Cholesterol: 55 mg
Sodium: 893 mg

Shellfish Paella

ᘒ

Paella is one of my favorite seafood dishes. But the expensive ingredients in it make it a luxury. Therefore, I suggest serving this dish for special occasions.

Even though the saffron called for is costly, nothing else gives the authentic taste and spectacular yellow color of this classic Spanish recipe. Many people use turmeric to achieve a similar color but, unfortunately, no other spice comes close to the taste of saffron.

For the best color, add a mixture of yellow, red, and green bell peppers.

8 fresh clams, scrubbed
2 tablespoons salt
2 tablespoons cornmeal
2 tablespoons extra-virgin olive oil
4 cloves garlic, pressed or minced
2 medium-size onions, chopped (3 cups)
2 or 3 small bell peppers, cut into strips (1 ½ cups)
2 cups raw white rice

½ cup finely chopped fresh parsley
Two 8-ounce bottles clam juice
2 cups dry white wine
One 8-ounce can tomato sauce
1 teaspoon salt
¼ cup fresh lemon juice
¼ teaspoon saffron
1 pound bay scallops
1 cup frozen peas, thawed
One 4-ounce jar sliced pimientos, undrained
8 large shrimp, peeled and deveined, with tails left on

1. First clean the clams: Place them in a large bowl and cover with cold water that has been mixed with 2 tablespoons salt. Sprinkle the cornmeal over the top and refrigerate for 3 to 12 hours. Drain and rinse thoroughly with clean water. This procedure will whiten the shells, remove the sand, and cause the clams to eject the black material in their stomachs.

2. Preheat the oven to 350° F.

3. Heat the olive oil in a flameproof paella pan or a large, ovenproof skillet. Add the garlic, onions, and bell peppers, and cook, stirring, over medium heat for 5 minutes. Add the rice and parsley and stir until the rice is well coated with oil.

4. Add the clam juice, wine, tomato sauce, salt, lemon juice, and saffron. Mix well and bring to a boil. Cover and place in the preheated oven and bake until all the liquid is absorbed, 1 hour and 15 minutes.

5. Remove from the oven and stir in the scallops, peas, and pimientos. Turn off the oven and return the paella to the oven to keep warm while cooking the shrimp and clams. Do not leave in the oven more than 5 minutes.

6. Steam the clams and shrimp, covered, over simmering water until the clams open and the shrimp turns from translucent to opaque, about 2 to 3 minutes. Do not overcook. Return any unopened clams to steamer and continue to steam until they open.

7. To serve, spoon 1 ¼ cups of the rice mixture on each of eight plates and top each serving with a shrimp and a clam; or arrange the clams and shrimp on top of the paella, place the pan in the center of the table, and let the guests help themselves.

Makes 8 servings

Each serving contains approximately
Calories: 375
Fat: 6 g
Cholesterol: 75 mg
Sodium: 930 mg

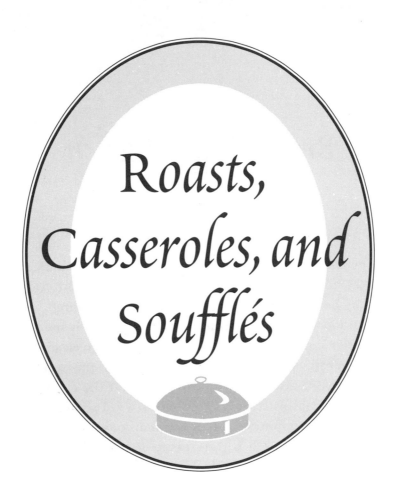

Roasts,
Casseroles, and
Soufflés

Brown Bag Chicken

ᠵᠣ

This incredibly easy meal takes only about 10 minutes to assemble and uses virtually every ingredient you bring home from the market to make it—including the bag! Cooking the chicken in the bag makes it much prettier and more tender, and it keeps the oven clean.

You can vary the vegetables and herbs in this recipe to suit your taste, and you can even stuff the chicken with your favorite dressing if you prefer. I sometimes de-fat the drippings, add an equal amount of nonfat milk, and thicken it with a teaspoon or two of cornstarch for a tasty fat-free chicken gravy.

One 3- to 4-pound frying chicken
$^1\!/_2$ teaspoon seasoned salt
$^1\!/_2$ teaspoon freshly ground black pepper
$^1\!/_4$ teaspoon garlic powder
Several sprigs fresh thyme; or 1 teaspoon dried thyme, crushed
1 medium-size onion, quartered
4 small red potatoes (1 pound total), halved
4 small carrots, peeled
One 10-ounce box frozen peas, unthawed

1. Place only one rack in the oven near the bottom so that the bag cannot come in contact with an upper rack or the heating elements on the top of the oven. Preheat the oven to 400° F.

2. Wash the chicken, inside and out, and pat dry. Rub the chicken with the salt, pepper, and garlic powder. Stuff the chicken with the thyme and onion. Place it, breast side up, in a 9 × 13-inch baking dish. Place the potatoes and carrots around the chicken and sprinkle the frozen peas over the top of the vegetables.

3. Place the dish inside of a large brown paper bag. Fold the ends of the bag over and staple it shut. Carefully place the bag-covered dish in the preheated oven, positioning it so that the bag cannot touch the heating elements. Bake for 1 ½ hours.

4. Remove the bag-covered dish from the oven and cut the bag open. Allow the chicken to rest for 10 minutes before removing the bag and carving the chicken. Serve the chicken with the onion, potatoes, carrots, and peas.

Makes 4 servings

Each serving contains approximately
Calories: 452
Fat: 9 g
Cholesterol: 101 mg
Sodium: 340 mg

Italian Chicken and Potatoes in a Bag

∿

Cooking in the new oven bags is a wonderful way to cut down on both the cooking time and the cleanup time. This spicy and very tasty chicken dish can be put together and baked in under an hour. If you prefer, you can leave out the potatoes and serve the chicken breasts and sauce over pasta or rice.

One 14 × 20-inch oven bag
2 tablespoons all-purpose flour
½ teaspoon dried rosemary, crushed
One 14 or 16-ounce jar spicy red pepper pasta sauce
½ cup chopped fresh parsley
4 bone-in, skinless chicken breast halves, all visible fat removed
1 large red bell pepper, seeds and membranes removed, chopped
8 new potatoes (1 pound total), peeled and thinly sliced

1. Preheat the oven to 350° F.

2. Put the flour and rosemary in the oven bag and shake to coat the inside of the bag.

3. Add the pasta sauce and parsley to the bag, squeezing it to blend the ingredients. Add the chicken, bell pepper, and potatoes, turning the bag to coat them with the sauce. Close the bag with the nylon tie (that is enclosed in the box with the oven bags) and place the bag in a 9 × 13-inch baking dish. Make sure the chicken breasts are in an even layer. Cut six ½-inch slits in the top of the bag and place the baking dish in the preheated oven. Bake until potatoes are tender, about 40 minutes.

4. Remove the dish from the oven and cut the top of the bag open to serve the chicken.

Makes 4 servings

Each serving contains approximately
Calories: 280
Fat: 3 g
Cholesterol: 72 mg
Sodium: 394 mg

Power-Saving Roast Beef with Root Vegetables

ʒ

This roast recipe is great for entertaining because you can practically finish preparing your meal two hours before you expect your guests to arrive.

One 3-pound triangle- or watermelon-cut beef roast, all visible
    fat removed
1 clove garlic
$1/2$ teaspoon dried oregano, crushed
$1/2$ teaspoon salt
$1/2$ teaspoon freshly ground black pepper
8 small potatoes (1 pound total), peeled and halved
8 medium-size carrots, peeled and halved
2 medium-size onions, quartered
$1/2$ cup water, wine, or beer

1. Preheat the oven to 500° F.

2. Rub the roast with garlic. Sprinkle it with the oregano, salt, and pepper. Place the roast in a roasting pan or a Dutch oven and add all the vegetables, cut side down, and the liquid.

3. Put the pan in the preheated oven for 30 minutes for rare roast beef or 35 minutes for medium-rare. Turn off the oven. Do not open the oven door for exactly 1 ½ hours.

4. Remove the roasting pan from the oven and allow the roast to stand for 10 minutes before slicing.

Makes 8 servings

Each serving contains approximately
Calories: 375
Fat: 8 g
Cholesterol: 103 mg
Sodium: 263 mg

Roasted Pork and Vegetables

❧

This easy-to-make one-dish meal is also a "one-pan" meal and therefore easy to clean up as well.

---

3 large sweet potatoes (1 ½ pounds total), peeled and cut into
  1-inch cubes
3 medium-size carrots, cut into ¾-inch rounds
1 medium-size onion, cut into 1-inch chunks
1 pound pork tenderloin, all visible fat removed, cut into 1-inch cubes
2 cloves garlic, pressed or minced
½ teaspoon dried rosemary, crushed
¼ teaspoon salt
¼ teaspoon freshly ground black pepper
⅓ cup fat-free chicken stock
1 tablespoon extra-virgin olive oil

1. Preheat the oven to 400° F.

2. Combine the sweet potatoes, carrots, onion, pork, garlic, rosemary, salt, and pepper in a roasting pan. Add the stock and olive oil and mix well. Spread out the mixture evenly over the bottom of the pan.

3. Place the pan in the preheated oven. Bake, stirring every 15 minutes, until the carrots and sweet potatoes are tender when pierced with a fork, 50 minutes.

Makes four 1 ¹/₂-cup servings

Each serving contains approximately
Calories: 339
Fat: 7 g
Cholesterol: 74 mg
Sodium: 244 mg

Southwestern Eggplant Casserole

⁊

This casserole makes a tasty and inexpensive buffet dish. Although it makes a meal by itself, I also like to serve it with a tossed green salad and low-fat baked corn chips.

---

1 large, unpeeled eggplant, cut into $\frac{1}{2}$-inch slices
1 tablespoon extra-virgin olive oil
One 15-ounce can tomato sauce
One 4-ounce can diced green chilies
1 medium-size onion, thinly sliced
$\frac{1}{2}$ teaspoon ground cumin
$\frac{1}{2}$ teaspoon garlic salt
$\frac{1}{2}$ teaspoon freshly ground black pepper
$\frac{1}{8}$ teaspoon red-pepper flakes
8 corn tortillas
6 ounces reduced-fat sharp Cheddar cheese, grated (1 $\frac{1}{2}$ cups)

1. Preheat the oven to 400° F. Spray a 9 × 13-inch baking dish with nonstick vegetable spray.

2. Spray the eggplant slices on both sides with nonstick vegetable spray. Place them in the prepared baking dish and bake in the preheated oven until soft, about 20 minutes. Remove from the oven. Reduce the oven temperature to 350° F.

3. While the eggplant is baking, combine all the remaining ingredients, except the tortillas and cheese, in a medium-size saucepan and bring to a boil over medium heat. Reduce the heat to low and cook, covered, for 15 minutes.

4. Remove half of the cooked eggplant from the baking dish, leaving a layer of eggplant slices on the bottom. Place 4 of the tortillas over the eggplant. Spoon half of the sauce over the eggplant in the dish. Top the sauce with half of the cheese. Top the cheese with the remaining eggplant, remaining tortillas, sauce, and cheese. Bake in the preheated oven until bubbly and lightly browned, about 30 minutes.

Makes 6 servings

Each serving contains approximately
Calories: 240
Fat: 9 g
Cholesterol: 24 mg
Sodium: 996 mg

Eggplant Parmesan

❧

This delicious eggplant dish is perfect for dinner on a cold winter night. It is ideal for potluck parties because it's a one-dish meal that can be easily transported. Also, it can be assembled ahead of time and then baked just before serving. Leftovers can be frozen and then thawed in a microwave for future meals or snacks.

If you are in a hurry, you can omit salting and draining the eggplant and simply cook the whole eggplant on a paper towel in a microwave oven until it is soft to the touch, about 6 to 7 minutes. When it is cool enough to handle, peel it and slice into 1/2-inch rounds. To bake the finished dish, microwave it, covered, on medium until hot and bubbly, 15 to 17 minutes.

However, when time permits, I prefer to salt and drain the eggplant to remove any bitterness that could affect the taste of the final dish. I also prefer to bake it in a standard oven so that the top is lightly browned.

---

1 large eggplant, about 1 pound
1 slice whole-wheat bread, torn into small pieces
1/4 cup freshly grated Parmesan cheese

2 cups low-fat pasta sauce
½ teaspoon dried oregano, crushed
8 ounces mozzarella cheese, grated

1. Peel the eggplant and cut horizontally into ½-inch slices. Lightly salt the eggplant slices and place them in a bowl. Cover and allow to stand for 1 hour to get rid of any bitterness. Drain the liquid and rinse the eggplant thoroughly. Steam the rinsed eggplant slices, covered, over simmering water or microwave them until they are tender and can be easily pierced with a fork, 3 to 4 minutes steamed; about 2 minutes microwaved. Set aside.

2. Preheat the oven to 350° F. Spray an 8 × 8 or a 7 × 11-inch baking dish with nonstick vegetable spray.

3. Place the bread and Parmesan cheese in a food processor or a blender and process until the bread is the consistency of gravel.

4. Combine the pasta sauce and oregano and mix well. Spoon half of the pasta sauce in the bottom of the prepared baking dish. Top the sauce with half of the cooked eggplant slices. Top the eggplant with half of the bread crumb and Parmesan cheese mixture and half of the mozzarella cheese. Repeat the layers.

5. Bake in the preheated oven for 30 minutes. Allow to stand for 5 minutes before serving.

Makes 4 servings

Each serving contains approximately
Calories: 269
Fat: 12 g
Cholesterol: 38 mg
Sodium: 810 mg

Southwestern Bread Pudding

ॐ

This spicy bread pudding makes a wonderful vegetarian brunch or lunch on its own. It also can be served as an entree or a side dish with fish, poultry, or meat.

---

9 cups cubed corn bread (or 12 slices whole-grain bread, cubed)
1 ¹/₂ cups vegetable stock
¹/₄ cup chopped fresh cilantro
¹/₄ cup chopped green onions (scallions), including the green tops
1 medium-size onion, chopped (1 ¹/₂ cups)
3 cloves garlic, pressed or minced
One 7-ounce can diced green chilies
2 tablespoons dried Sonoma tomato bits
1 cup corn kernels
¹/₄ teaspoon ground cumin
¹/₄ teaspoon salt (omit if using salted stock)
¹/₄ teaspoon freshly ground black pepper
4 ounces reduced-fat Monterey Jack cheese, grated (1 cup)

1. Preheat the oven to 350° F. Spray a 2-quart casserole with nonstick vegetable spray and set aside.

2. Combine the bread, stock, cilantro, and green onions in a large bowl and mix well. Set aside.

3. Combine the onion and garlic in a medium-size nonstick saucepan and cook, covered, over low heat, adding a little water if necessary to prevent scorching, until the onion is translucent, about 10 minutes. Add the chilies, tomato bits, corn, cumin, salt, and pepper and mix well. Cook, uncovered, stirring frequently, for 5 minutes. Remove from the heat and add to the bread mixture. Add the cheese to the bowl and mix all the ingredients together.

4. Spoon the mixture into the prepared casserole and bake until the top is a golden brown, about 45 minutes.

Makes 6 servings

Each serving contains approximately
Calories: 226
Fat: 6 g
Cholesterol: 15 mg
Sodium: 845 mg

Potato, Mushroom, and Camembert Gratin

∽

Camembert has a distinctly different taste that blends perfectly with the other flavors in this simple French country gratin. This now-famous cow's milk cheese has a fine-textured rind and a smooth, creamy center. Select Camembert that is plump and soft to the touch to insure against overripeness.

This dish is perfect for a light and hearty summer lunch or supper, served with just a tossed green salad.

---

2 slices whole-wheat bread
10 good-sized red new potatoes (1 ½ pounds total), scrubbed but
    not peeled
2 ounces (3 cups) dried mushrooms
8 ounces fairly firm Camembert, rind removed, diced
½ teaspoon salt
½ teaspoon freshly ground black pepper
One 12-ounce can evaporated skim milk
1 tablespoon corn-oil margarine, melted

3 cloves garlic, minced
1 ½ teaspoons dried thyme, crushed
3 tablespoons freshly grated Parmesan cheese

1. Tear the bread into pieces and process it in a food processor until the bread is the consistency of fine gravel. Set aside.

2. Slice the potatoes into very thin pieces, about ⅛-inch thick. Place them in a large bowl of cold water and soak for 30 minutes, changing the water twice. Drain them and pat dry.

3. Meanwhile, place the mushrooms in a bowl and cover with hot water. Allow to soak for 30 minutes. Drain; remove the stems, and cut the caps into thin strips.

4. Preheat the oven to 425° F. Spray a gratin dish or shallow glass baking dish about 10 inches across with nonstick vegetable spray.

5. Layer one-third of the potato slices in the prepared dish. Lay half the mushrooms and half the cheese evenly over the top. Season with ¼ teaspoon of the salt and pepper. Add another third of the potatoes and top with the remaining mushrooms and cheese. Season with the remaining ¼ teaspoon of the salt and pepper. Arrange the remaining potato slices on top. Combine the milk, margarine, garlic, and thyme and pour over the potatoes, pushing down so all the liquid is absorbed. Cover the dish tightly with foil and bake for 30 minutes.

6. Combine the Parmesan cheese and bread crumbs. Remove the foil and sprinkle the cheese and bread crumbs over the potatoes. Place the dish on a rack in the bottom third of the oven and bake until the potatoes are very tender and the top and bottom are crusty and dark brown, 30 to 40 minutes longer.

Makes 10 servings

Each serving contains approximately
Calories: 245
Fat: 8 g
Cholesterol: 19 mg
Sodium: 425 mg

Asparagus au Gratin

ॐ

I like to serve this dish for brunch or lunch, garnished with orange and grapefruit sections. It also makes a good entree or a side dish for grilled fish, poultry, or meat.

---

1 pound fresh asparagus, trimmed
About ³/₄ cup nonfat milk
1 tablespoon corn-oil margarine
3 tablespoons all-purpose flour
¹/₂ teaspoon salt
4 large hard-cooked eggs, yolks discarded and whites sliced
3 slices whole-wheat toast, cut into ¹/₄-inch strips
3 ounces reduced-fat Monterey Jack cheese, grated (³/₄ cup)
Paprika

1. Preheat the oven to 350°F.

2. Arrange the asparagus in a large skillet, add 1 cup water, and bring to a boil over high heat. Reduce the heat to medium and boil gently until tender, about 5 minutes. Drain ¹/₂ cup cooking liquid into a 2-cup measure and add enough of the milk to make 1 ¹/₂ cups total liquid; set aside.

3. Melt the margarine in a medium-size saucepan over medium heat. Add the flour and cook, stirring constantly, for 1 minute. Slowly stir in the milk mixture and salt, and cook, stirring constantly until the mixture boils and thickens, about 5 minutes. Remove the sauce from the heat and set aside.

4. Alternate, in a 1 ½-quart casserole, layers of the hard-cooked egg whites, toast, cheese, and asparagus. Cover with the sauce and sprinkle with the paprika. Bake in preheated oven until the cheese melts, about 10 minutes.

Makes 4 servings

Each serving contains approximately
Calories: 211
Fat: 9 g
Cholesterol: 19 mg
Sodium: 573 mg

Cabbage and Cheese Casserole

∽

This simple, rich-tasting dish makes a wonderfully satisfying and versatile vegetarian lunch or dinner. It can also serve as an entree or a side dish, or you can add leftover fish, poultry, or meat to the casserole if you prefer to serve it to nonvegetarians.

I have suggested that you add caraway seed because I particularly like their taste with cabbage. Instead of caraway you could also use rye bread in place of the whole-wheat called for in the recipe and achieve much the same taste. This dish is even good served cold and makes an unusual salad or condiment.

---

1 medium-size head cabbage, shredded and cooked until tender
¼ cup nonfat milk
One 10 ¾-ounce can low-fat cream of celery soup
½ teaspoon freshly ground black pepper
½ teaspoon caraway seeds (optional)
4 ounces reduced-fat sharp Cheddar cheese, grated (1 cup)
2 slices whole-wheat bread, torn into pieces
2 tablespoons corn-oil margarine, melted

1. Preheat the oven to 350° F. Spray a 7 × 11-inch baking dish with nonstick vegetable spray. Spread the cooked cabbage in the bottom of the dish.

2. Combine the milk, soup, pepper, and caraway seeds, if using, in a medium-size bowl and mix well. Stir in ⅓ cup of the cheese and spoon evenly over the cabbage.

3. Put the bread in a food processor or a blender and process until the consistency of gravel. Add the margarine and mix well.

4. Sprinkle the bread and remaining ⅔ cup of the cheese over the top of the dish and bake in the preheated oven until bubbly, about 15 minutes.

Makes 4 servings

Each serving contains approximately
Calories: 282
Fat: 15 g
Cholesterol: 28 mg
Sodium: 619 mg

Broccoli and Cheese Casserole

᧒

This recipe is a revision of a reader's favorite dish that required very little change other than substituting nonfat and reduced-fat ingredients for the high-fat items called for in the original recipe. It can be made ahead of time and then baked just before serving.

1 tablespoon corn-oil margarine
1 large onion, chopped (2 cups)
1 rib celery, chopped ($^{1}/_{4}$ cup)
Two 16-ounce bags frozen chopped broccoli, thawed
6 cups cooked white rice
One 10 $^{3}/_{4}$-ounce can low-fat condensed cream of mushroom soup
One 10 $^{3}/_{4}$-ounce can low-fat condensed cream of chicken soup
1 $^{1}/_{4}$ cups nonfat milk
One 8 $^{1}/_{4}$-ounce jar light Cheez Whiz; or 8 ounces light Velveeta, cubed
One 8-ounce can sliced water chestnuts, drained
1 tablespoon butter-flavored sprinkles
1 teaspoon salt
2 ounces reduced-fat sharp Cheddar cheese, grated ($^{1}/_{2}$ cup)

1. Preheat the oven to 350° F. Spray two 8-cup casseroles or deep baking dishes with nonstick vegetable spray; set aside.

2. In a large, nonstick skillet, melt the margarine over medium heat. Add the onion and celery and cook, stirring, until soft, about 5 minutes.

3. In a large bowl, place the cooked vegetables and all the other ingredients, except the Cheddar cheese. Mix well and divide evenly between the two prepared dishes. Sprinkle the ¼ cup Cheddar cheese over each dish and bake in a preheated oven until hot and bubbly, 45 minutes.

Makes fourteen 1-cup servings

Each serving contains approximately
Calories: 215
Fat: 6 g
Cholesterol: 16 mg
Sodium: 763 mg

Broccoli and Rice Casserole

⁊

Like the recipe for Broccoli and Cheese Casserole (page 150), this recipe required little revision other than the substitution of low-fat ingredients.

One 6.2-ounce box fast-cooking long-grain and wild rice with seasoning packet
12 ounces nonfat cream cheese
Two 10 ³/₄-ounce cans condensed low-fat cream of mushroom soup
4 ounces reduced-fat sharp Cheddar cheese, grated (1 cup)
1 medium-size onion, chopped (1 ¹/₂ cups)
Three 10-ounce packages frozen chopped broccoli, thawed

1. Preheat the oven to 350° F. Spray a 3-quart casserole with non-stick vegetable spray and set aside.

2. Cook the rice according to package directions, omitting any butter or margarine called for. (This takes about 5 minutes.)

3. While the rice is cooking, combine the cream cheese and soup in a large bowl and mix them until smooth and creamy. Add the Cheddar cheese, onion, and broccoli and mix well. Add the cooked rice and again mix well.

4. Spoon the mixture into the prepared casserole and bake in the preheated oven until the top is a golden brown, about 50 minutes.

Makes twelve 1-cup servings

Each serving contains approximately
Calories: 158
Fat: 4 g
Cholesterol: 15 mg
Sodium: 665 mg

Shrimp Florentine Casserole

ॐ

If you're using frozen shrimp for this dish, allow them to thaw completely before cooking them to ensure the best texture. When you cook any frozen fish or seafood without first thawing it, the texture tends to be a bit mushy.

---

1 tablespoon corn-oil margarine
2 tablespoons all-purpose flour
One 12-ounce can evaporated skim milk, heated until bubbles appear
*   around the edge*
$\frac{1}{8}$ teaspoon salt
$\frac{1}{8}$ teaspoon ground white pepper
$\frac{1}{8}$ teaspoon ground nutmeg
$\frac{1}{2}$ cup shredded low-fat mozzarella cheese
1 cup dry white wine
1 pound medium-size shrimp, shelled and deveined
2 cups cooked rice
One 16-ounce package frozen chopped spinach, cooked and
*   squeezed dry*
2 tablespoons freshly grated Parmesan cheese

1. Preheat the oven to 350° F. Spray a 7 × 11-inch baking dish with nonstick vegetable spray.

2. Melt the margarine in a saucepan over medium-low heat. Add the flour and cook, stirring constantly for 2 minutes. Do not brown. Add the hot milk, all at once, stirring constantly with a wire whisk. Stir in the salt, pepper, and nutmeg and continue to simmer, stirring frequently, until slightly thickened, about 10 minutes. Remove from the heat and stir in the mozzarella cheese. Set the mixture aside.

3. Bring the white wine to a boil in a small skillet or saucepan. Add the shrimp and cook until they turn pink and opaque, about 2 to 3 minutes.

4. Combine the rice and spinach and spread the mixture evenly over the bottom of the prepared dish. Place the cooked shrimp on top of the spinach and pour the shrimp liquid over the top. Spoon the milk and cheese mixture over the top of the shrimp. Sprinkle the Parmesan cheese evenly over the top of the dish.

5. Place the dish in the preheated oven and bake until it is heated through, about 10 minutes. Then place it under the broiler to lightly brown the top.

Makes 4 servings

Each serving contains approximately
Calories: 428
Fat: 9 g
Cholesterol: 143 mg
Sodium: 574 mg

Lemon Bass and Pasta Casserole

᎒

If you feel you want a vegetable with this casserole, you can add a cooked green vegetable or serve it with a cold marinated vegetable salad.

1 pound skinless bass fillets
$^1/_2$ teaspoon salt
$^1/_4$ teaspoon freshly ground black pepper
8 ounces pasta shells, cooked al dente
1 tablespoon extra-virgin olive oil
$^1/_2$ cup dry vermouth
1 $^1/_2$ tablespoons cornstarch
One 12-ounce can evaporated skim milk
2 tablespoon sherry
1 tablespoon grated lemon zest
2 tablespoons fresh lemon juice
$^1/_4$ cup freshly grated Parmesan cheese

1. Wash the fish and pat it dry. Remove any remaining bones with tweezers. Sprinkle both sides of the fish with the salt and pepper. Set aside.

2. Toss the hot, cooked pasta with the olive oil and put it in a 2- to 3-quart casserole dish. Cover to keep warm and set aside.

3. Pour the vermouth into a large skillet and bring to a simmer over medium heat. Add the fish and cook until it turns from translucent to opaque throughout, about 3 to 5 minutes. Carefully remove the fish from the pan and place it on top of the pasta. Re-cover the casserole.

4. Combine the cornstarch and ¼ cup of the milk and stir until the cornstarch is completely dissolved. Add it to the liquid in the skillet. Add the remaining milk and the sherry, lemon zest, and juice, and mix well. Bring it to a boil over medium heat, reduce the heat to medium-low, and cook, stirring constantly, until slightly thickened, about 2 minutes.

5. Pour the sauce over the fish and pasta in the casserole. Sprinkle the Parmesan cheese evenly over the top. Place the dish under a broiler until a golden brown.

Makes 4 servings

Each serving contains approximately
Calories: 475
Fat: 7 g
Cholesterol: 71 mg
Sodium: 600 mg

Red Snapper Almondine au Gratin

ꙅ

This is an easy-to-make and delicious last-minute dinner. If you prefer, you can toast sunflower seeds instead of almonds to top this dish. Also, you can substitute couscous for the rice.

¼ cup chopped raw almonds
2 cups cooked rice
1 pound red snapper fillets
½ teaspoon salt
¼ teaspoon freshly ground black pepper
1 tablespoon fresh lemon juice
One 14 ½-ounce can crushed tomatoes
2 ounces grated reduced-fat Monterey Jack cheese (½ cup)

1. Preheat the oven to 350° F.

2. Place the almonds in the preheated oven and bake, stirring once or twice, until golden brown, about 10 minutes. Watch them carefully because they burn easily. Set aside. (Toasting sunflower seeds takes only about 5 minutes.)

3. Spread the rice evenly over the bottom of a 7 × 11-inch baking dish. Sprinkle both sides of the fish with the salt and pepper. Place it on top of the rice and sprinkle with the lemon juice. Cover and bake in the preheated oven until opaque throughout, about 20 minutes. Remove the dish from the oven and spread the tomatoes evenly over the top. Sprinkle the toasted almonds over the tomatoes and then sprinkle the cheese over the top of the dish. Place it back in the oven just until the cheese is melted.

Makes 4 servings

Each serving contains approximately
Calories: 556
Fat: 13 g
Cholesterol: 141 mg
Sodium: 830 mg

Corn and Tuna Casserole

⌇

If you are making this dish in the summer when fresh corn is available, by all means use it to replace the can of corn kernels called for in this recipe. Also, after cutting the corn kernels off the cob, scrape the cob with the dull side of a knife to "milk" the liquid left in the cob and add it to the casserole for flavor.

½ cup yellow cornmeal
½ cup unbleached all-purpose flour
½ teaspoon baking soda
1 teaspoon salt
2 tablespoons sugar
½ cup liquid egg substitute
One 15-ounce can unsalted cream-style corn
One 15-ounce can unsalted whole-kernel corn, undrained
One 6-ounce can water-packed white tuna, drained
1 cup nonfat sour cream
½ cup buttermilk
1 tablespoon corn-oil margarine, melted

1. Preheat the oven to 350° F. Spray a 2-quart casserole dish with nonstick vegetable spray and set aside.

2. Combine the cornmeal, flour, baking soda, salt, and sugar in a bowl and mix well. Add all the remaining ingredients, mix well, and spoon into the prepared casserole. Bake, uncovered, in the preheated oven until a knife inserted in the center comes out clean, about 1 hour.

Makes eight ³/₄-cup servings

Each serving contains approximately
Calories: 233
Fat: 3 g
Cholesterol: 5 mg
Sodium: 512 mg

Cottage Cheese Loaf

ॐ

This recipe is ideal for using up leftover cooked chicken or turkey. Just chop it up and mix it in with the cottage cheese. If you want to make this a vegetarian meal, substitute low-fat cream of mushroom or celery soup for the cream of chicken called for in this recipe.

1 quart nonfat cottage cheese
1 cup liquid egg substitute
2 large egg whites, lightly beaten
One 10 ³/₄-ounce can condensed low-fat cream of chicken soup
5 cups Cheerios toasted oat cereal
1 large onion, diced (2 cups)
¹/₃ cup shelled walnuts, chopped and toasted
¹/₂ teaspoon salt
¹/₄ teaspoon freshly ground black pepper

1. Preheat the oven to 350° F. Spray a 9 × 13-inch baking dish with nonstick vegetable spray and set aside.

2. Combine the cottage cheese, egg substitute, egg whites, and soup in a large bowl and mix well. Stir in all the remaining ingredients and spoon into the prepared baking dish.

3. Bake in the preheated oven for 1 hour. Remove from the oven and allow to cool for 10 minutes before serving.

Makes eight 1-cup servings

Each serving contains approximately
Calories: 233
Fat: 6 g
Cholesterol: 209 mg
Sodium: 902 mg

Portola Valley Chicken

ᔰ

This dish is also good made with canned tuna. Just substitute two 6-ounce cans or one 12-ounce can of drained, water-packed white tuna for the chicken breasts.

One 10 ³/₄-ounce can condensed low-fat cream of chicken soup
¹/₂ cup cold water
¹/₂ cup fat-free mayonnaise
¹/₂ teaspoon curry powder
¹/₂ cup raw brown rice
One 10-ounce package frozen chopped spinach, thawed, undrained
4 boneless, skinless chicken breast halves (1 pound)
¹/₃ cup freshly grated Parmesan cheese

1. Preheat the oven to 350° F. Spray a 7 × 11-inch baking dish with nonstick vegetable spray and set aside.

2. Combine the soup, water, mayonnaise, and curry powder and mix well.

3. Sprinkle the rice over the bottom of the prepared baking dish. Layer the spinach evenly over the top of the rice. Cover the spinach with half of the soup mixture, then top with the chicken, then the remaining soup mixture. Sprinkle the cheese over the top and bake, uncovered, until bubbly and golden brown, 1 hour.

Makes 4 servings

Each serving contains approximately
Calories: 323
Fat: 5 g
Cholesterol: 79 mg
Sodium: 793 mg

Tortilla Casserole

ॐ

This recipe is sure to be a favorite on the potluck circuit and is also great for tailgate parties.

One 10 ¾-ounce can low-fat condensed cream of chicken soup
½ cup nonfat milk
½ cup nonfat sour cream
1 medium-size onion, grated
One 4-ounce can diced green chilies
12 corn tortillas, cut into thin strips
Two 10-ounce cans water-packed chunk white chicken, drained and shredded
4 ounces reduced-fat sharp Cheddar cheese, grated (1 cup)

1. Preheat the oven to 350° F. Spray a 9 × 13-inch baking dish with nonstick vegetable spray and set aside.

2. In a large bowl, combine the soup, milk, sour cream, onion, and chilies and mix thoroughly.

3. Spread half of the tortilla strips in the bottom of the prepared dish. Spread half of the chicken over the strips, then half the soup mixture. Repeat the layers, and sprinkle the cheese over the top.

4. Bake the dish in the preheated oven until hot and bubbly, about 30 minutes.

Makes 8 servings

Each serving contains approximately
Calories: 286
Fat: 7 g
Cholesterol: 47 mg
Sodium: 622 mg

Baked Chicken and Rice with Apricot Sauce

∿

This dish is good both hot and cold. The reader who sent it to me said that she likes it best cold. In the summertime she makes it the day before and serves it as a cold luncheon salad plate garnished with fresh fruit.

8 boneless, skinless chicken breast halves (2 pounds)
One 10-ounce jar fruit-only apricot preserves
One 1-ounce package dry onion soup mix
One 8-ounce bottle nonfat Russian or Catalina salad dressing
4 cups cooked rice

1. Preheat the oven to 325° F. Spray a 9 × 13-inch baking dish with nonstick vegetable spray.

2. Place the chicken breasts in the bottom of the prepared dish. Combine the preserves, soup mix, and salad dressing and spread them evenly over the chicken.

3. Bake in the preheated oven until the chicken is no longer pink, about 1 hour. Serve each breast on ½ cup of the rice and spoon a little sauce over the top.

Makes 8 servings

Each serving contains approximately
Calories: 387
Fat: 5 g
Cholesterol: 86 mg
Sodium: 645 mg

Scalloped Chicken

~

This recipe can also be made with turkey if you're looking for a way to use up the rest of the holiday bird.

2 ribs celery and leaves, finely chopped
6 green onions (scallions), including green tops, finely chopped
4 sprigs parsley, finely chopped
2 ½ cups low-fat packaged stuffing mix
One 14 ½-ounce can fat-free chicken stock
2 tablespoons cornstarch
½ cup nonfat milk
⅛ teaspoon salt
3 cups cooked chicken, without skin (1 ½ pounds uncooked), cut
    into bite-size pieces
⅓ cup dry bread crumbs
1 tablespoon corn-oil margarine, melted

1. Heat ¼ cup of the water in a small skillet over low heat. Add the celery, green onions, and parsley and cook for 5 minutes. Place the stuffing mix in a large bowl, add the vegetables and their cooking liquid, plus an additional 3 tablespoons of the water, and mix lightly with a fork.

2. Preheat the oven to 375° F. Spray a 9 × 13-inch baking dish with nonstick vegetable spray. Place the stuffing mixture in the bottom of the dish and set it aside.

3. To make the sauce, warm the stock in a medium-size saucepan over medium heat. Dissolve the cornstarch in the milk and add to the broth. Cook slowly, stirring occasionally, until the mixture thickens slightly. Stir in the salt.

4. Pour half of the sauce, about 1 cup, over the stuffing mixture. Place the chicken pieces on top of the sauce and cover with the remaining sauce. Combine the dry bread crumbs with the margarine and sprinkle over the top.

5. Bake, uncovered, in the preheated oven until a golden brown and heated through, about 20 minutes.

Makes six 1-cup servings

Each serving contains approximately
Calories: 290
Fat: 9 g
Cholesterol: 65 mg
Sodium: 390 mg

Larry's "Canned" Chicken

⁊

When I told my friend, Larry Case, that I was working on a book of one-dish meals, he told me he would give me a recipe for his favorite quick-and-easy chicken dish with his "secret sauce." He is such a superb cook that I was amazed to discover that the "secret" of his sauce in this truly delicious dish is a can of soup.

You can either bake this dish with the rice as I have done in this recipe or bake the chicken by itself and serve it over cooked rice, pasta, potatoes, or steamed vegetables. You can change the flavor range by substituting cream of mushroom or celery soup for the cream of chicken soup. Also, you can add sautéed garlic, onions, or mushrooms for variety and any of your favorite herbs or spices.

4 boneless, skinless chicken thighs or breast halves
2 cups cooked rice
$1/2$ cup water
One 10 $3/4$-ounce can condensed low-fat cream of chicken soup
2 tablespoons sherry
$1/4$ teaspoon freshly ground black pepper

1. Preheat the oven to 325° F. Spray a 7 × 11-inch baking dish with nonstick vegetable spray.

2. Brown the chicken in a medium-size, nonstick skillet over medium-high heat, about 5 minutes per side.

3. Spread the cooked rice evenly over the bottom of the prepared baking dish. Remove the chicken from the skillet and arrange it on top of the rice.

4. Add the water to the skillet and bring it to a boil over high heat, scraping up any browned bits, to deglaze it. Then add the soup and sherry and stir until smooth.

5. Pour the soup mixture over the chicken. Cover the dish tightly and bake in the preheated oven until tender, about 1 hour.

Makes 4 servings

Each serving contains approximately
Calories: 363
Fat: 11 g
Cholesterol: 88 mg
Sodium: 373 mg

Chicken and Artichoke Buffet

☙

This is a revision of a very high-fat recipe. My version
is still an extremely rich-tasting dish.

2 tablespoons plus 1 teaspoon corn-oil margarine
2 cloves garlic, pressed or minced
6 tablespoons unbleached all-purpose flour
1 ½ cups fat-free chicken stock
1 cup nonfat milk
¾ teaspoon salt (omit if using salted stock)
¼ teaspoon freshly ground black pepper
4 cups cooked wild rice
½ pound white mushrooms, sliced (2 cups)
10 green onions (scallions), including green tops, chopped
⅓ cup 2 percent low-fat milk
½ cup sherry
6 boneless, skinless chicken breast halves, cooked and sliced
    into ½ × 1 ½-inch strips (4 cups)
Four 7-ounce or two 14-ounce cans water-packed artichoke hearts,
    drained and quartered
6 ounces Canadian bacon, chopped
1 pound carrots, cut into 1-inch matchstick strips, steamed 4 minutes,
    and rinsed in cold water and drained

8 ounces part-skim mozzarella cheese, grated (2 cups)
2 tablespoons freshly grated Parmesan cheese

1. Preheat the oven to 350° F. Spray a 9 × 13-inch baking dish with nonstick vegetable spray.

2. Melt 2 tablespoons of the margarine in a medium-size saucepan. Add the garlic and cook it until it sizzles. Add the flour and stir it over medium heat for 2 minutes. Do not brown. Add the stock and milk and stir, using a wire whisk, over medium heat, until the mixture comes to a boil. Add the salt and pepper and continue to cook for 1 minute more. Measure out ¼ cup of the sauce and set the remainder aside.

3. Spread the ¼ cup sauce evenly over the bottom of the prepared dish. Spoon the rice over the sauce.

4. In a large, nonstick skillet, melt the additional teaspoon margarine. Add the mushrooms and green onions and cook, stirring, over medium heat until tender, about 5 minutes. Stir in the remaining sauce, low-fat milk, and sherry; mix well.

5. In a large bowl, combine the mushroom mixture, chicken, artichokes, bacon, carrots, and mozzarella. Mix well and spread over rice. Sprinkle with the Parmesan cheese.

6. Bake the dish, covered, in the preheated oven for 30 minutes. Uncover and bake until golden brown, 15 minutes more.

Makes ten 1 ¼-cup servings

Each serving contains approximately
Calories: 395
Fat: 14 g
Cholesterol: 69 mg
Sodium: 1,153 mg

Herbed Chicken on Vegetables and Rice

ॐ

The personality of any dish is largely dependent on the herbs and spices used. This recipe for Herbed Chicken on Vegetables and Rice is a perfect example. I have used oregano, which gives the dish an Italian overtone. You could make it seem more Greek by adding a little cinnamon to the herbs already called for. Or you could change the herbs and spices completely and make it taste French by using tarragon, Spanish with saffron, Asian with ginger and curry, Mexican with cumin and chili powder, or Thai by using basil and lemon grass.

1 ²/₃ cups fat-free chicken stock
¹/₄ teaspoon salt (omit if using salted stock)
¹/₄ teaspoon freshly ground black pepper
1 bay leaf
³/₄ cup raw brown rice
2 small zucchini, cut into matchstick strips (2 cups)
4 boneless, skinless chicken breast halves, all visible fat removed
1 teaspoon dried basil, crushed
¹/₂ teaspoon dried oregano, crushed

¹/₂ teaspoon dried thyme, crushed

8 plum tomatoes, peeled and diced; or one 28-ounce can ready-cut tomatoes

Parsley sprigs or fennel fern, for garnish (optional)

Sauce

1 ¹/₂ cups chopped fresh fennel, including fern (6 ounces)

1 medium-size onion, chopped (1 ¹/₂ cups)

2 cloves garlic, halved

2 tablespoons water

¹/₂ teaspoon ground anise seed

2 tablespoons extra-virgin olive oil

1. Preheat the oven to 350° F. Spray a 7 × 11-inch baking dish with nonstick vegetable spray.

2. Combine the stock, salt, pepper, and the bay leaf in a medium-size saucepan and bring to a boil over medium-high heat. Add the rice, reduce heat to low, and cook, covered, until the rice is tender and all the liquid is absorbed, about 45 minutes.

3. Remove and discard the bay leaf. Spoon the rice into the prepared baking dish and spread it evenly over the bottom of the dish. Spread the zucchini pieces evenly over the rice. Lightly salt and pepper both sides of the chicken breasts and place them on top of the zucchini. Sprinkle the herbs over the chicken. Spread the tomatoes evenly over the chicken. Sprinkle the parsley over the top.

4. Cover tightly with a lid or aluminum foil and bake in the preheated oven until the chicken is completely opaque, about 20 minutes. Do not overcook or the chicken will become tough.

5. While the chicken is cooking, make the sauce. Combine all the ingredients, except the olive oil, in a blender or food processor and purée. Pour the puréed mixture into a medium-size saucepan and bring to a boil over medium heat. Remove from the heat and pour it through a strainer, pressing it with the back of a spoon to extract all the liquid. Pour back into the saucepan. Whisk in the olive

oil, cover, and set aside to keep warm.

6. To serve, use a spatula to remove each serving, being careful to get the rice, chicken, and vegetables out intact and onto each plate. Pour one-quarter of the sauce over each serving and garnish, if desired, with the parsley sprigs or fennel fern.

Makes 4 servings

Each serving contains approximately
Calories: 427
Fat: 12 g
Cholesterol: 72 mg
Sodium: 305 mg

Herbs and Spice and Everything Nice

Herbs and spices are extremely important in a healthier approach to cooking. They contain practically no calories or sodium, and they are completely fat and cholesterol free. If you don't have many dried herbs and spices in your kitchen right now, start adding to your collection each time you go to the market. Always store them in a cool, dark place because sunlight will quickly destroy their intensity.

Also, it is a big help to alphabetize your herbs and spices. This may not seem important to you now, but as you acquire more of them, it can save a great deal of time and frustration when you don't have to look through all of them to find just one.

When using dried herbs and spices that are not powdered, it is important to crush them using a mortar and pestle to release their full flavor.

Southwestern Catfish en Papillote

❧

En papillote (pah-pee-yoht) is just a fancy, French way of describing food baked in a wrapping of parchment paper or aluminum foil. As the food bakes and lets off steam, the paper puffs up into a dome shape. Just before serving, the paper is slit and folded back to display the dish inside. This dramatic presentation is sure to get rave reviews from your guests.

It is a perfect one-dish meal for holiday entertaining because it can be made ahead of time and placed on baking sheets in the refrigerator until you are ready to bake it. Cleanup is a snap, too, because there are no greasy pans or food-encrusted plates to scrub.

Also, by using U.S. farm-raised catfish in this recipe, there is absolutely no worry about the origin of the fish or the consistency of taste. All farm-raised catfish are raised in a quality-controlled environment of clay-based ponds filled with pure fresh water pumped in from underground wells. The fish are fed a special high-protein grain that floats on the surface, causing them to feed on the top of the water instead of the bottom. The result is a mild, sweet-tasting fish that is low in fat, calories, and sodium and high in protein, vitamins, and minerals.

Four 5-ounce skinless catfish fillets
2 limes
1 medium-size onion, finely chopped (1 ½ cups)
2 cloves garlic, pressed or minced
One 7-ounce can diced green chilies
¼ teaspoon salt
½ teaspoon freshly ground black pepper
½ teaspoon ground cumin
2 teaspoons chili powder
One 15-ounce can pinto beans, drained
4 sheets parchment paper or aluminum foil (about 24 inches square)
1 cup fresh or frozen thawed corn kernels
2 small zucchini (8 ounces), cut into matchstick strips (2 cups)
4 plum tomatoes (8 ounces), peeled and diced (1 cup)
¼ cup chopped fresh cilantro
1 egg white (for sealing the parchment paper packages)
Salsa (optional)

1. Preheat the oven to 350° F.

2. Wash the catfish fillets with cold water, pat dry, and set in a shallow dish. Squeeze the juice of both limes over the fillets. Cover them and refrigerate until ready to use.

3. Combine the onion and garlic in a large, heavy saucepan and cook, covered, over low heat until the onion is translucent, 10 to 15 minutes, adding a little water if necessary to prevent scorching. Add the diced chilies, salt, pepper, cumin, and chili powder and cook for 3 more minutes. Add the beans and mix well. Set aside.

4. Cut the parchment paper or foil into large hearts by folding each piece of paper in half and then cutting the folded paper into a half-heart shape. Unfold the hearts, and spoon ½ cup of the bean mixture onto the center of one side of each heart. Top the beans with ¼ cup of the corn, a catfish fillet, ½ cup of the zucchini and ¼ cup of the tomato in that order. Top each serving with a tablespoon of the chopped cilantro.

5. To close the parchment hearts, brush the edges with the egg white. Then fold the empty half of the heart carefully over the contents, pressing the edges together. (If using foil, omit the egg white.) To seal each "package," fold the edges over, starting at the top with a small fold and continuing all the way around with overlapping folds, crimping the edges tightly with your fingers.

6. Place the packages on baking sheets, 2 per sheet, and bake in the preheated oven for 13 minutes.

7. To serve, place each package on a plate and cut a large X on the top. Fold back the corners exposing the contents. Pass the salsa to spoon over the top if desired.

Makes 4 servings

Each serving contains approximately
Calories: 404
Fat: 7 g
Cholesterol: 82 mg
Sodium: 829 mg

Turkey Sausage and Spinach Bake

⁊

This spicy, easy-to-make dish is great for buffet entertaining and for portable meals such as tailgate parties.

---

3 tablespoons chopped green onions (scallions), including the
   green tops
8 turkey sausage links (5 ¹/₂ ounces)
2 ounces reduced-fat sharp Cheddar cheese, grated (¹/₂ cup)
3 ounces reduced-fat Swiss cheese, grated (³/₄ cup)
1 teaspoon Italian seasoning
¹/₄ teaspoon garlic salt
One 10-ounce package frozen chopped spinach, thawed and
   squeezed dry
1 cup liquid egg substitute
4 large egg whites
1 cup low-fat milk
3 ounces reduced-fat cream cheese, cubed

1. Preheat the oven to 350° F. Spray a 10-inch quiche pan with nonstick vegetable spray.

2. Cook the green onion, stirring in 1 tablespoon water in a small, nonstick skillet over medium heat until soft. Place in a large mixing bowl.

3. Cook the sausage according to the package instructions; drain well, then slice into ½-inch pieces. Add the sausage to the green onions along with the Cheddar, Swiss, and Italian seasoning and garlic salt. Mix well and spread in the prepared pan.

4. Distribute the spinach over the top of the sausage mixture. Beat the egg substitute, egg whites, and milk together and pour over the spinach. Distribute the cream cheese over the top and bake until set, 40 to 45 minutes.

Makes 8 servings

Each serving contains approximately
Calories: 154
Fat: 9 g
Cholesterol: 32 mg
Sodium: 363 mg

Creamy Turkey and Broccoli

ॐ

This recipe is really a combination of convenience products that is surprisingly tasty and certainly easy to make.

_____

2 cups water
One 6-ounce package reduced-sodium stuffing mix
²/₃ cup canned french-fried onions
One 10-ounce package frozen broccoli spears, thawed and drained
One 1 ¹/₄-ounce package cheese sauce mix
1 cup nonfat milk
¹/₂ cup light sour cream
2 cups cooked and cubed turkey or chicken meat

1. Preheat the oven to 350° F. Spray a 9-inch round baking dish with nonstick vegetable spray and set it aside.

2. In a medium-size saucepan, combine the 2 cups water and the seasoning packet from the stuffing mix. Bring to a boil over high heat, reduce the heat to low, cover, and simmer 5 minutes. Stir in the stuffing, cover, and remove from the heat. Allow to stand for 5 minutes and then fluff with a fork. Stir in about ¹/₃ cup of the french-fried onions and spread the mixture over the bottom of the prepared dish.

Arrange the broccoli spears over the stuffing with the florets around the edge of the dish.

3. Put the cheese sauce mix in a medium-size saucepan. Gradually stir in the milk and cook over medium heat, stirring constantly, until the sauce thickens. Remove from the heat and stir in the sour cream and the turkey or chicken meat.

4. Pour the sauce mixture over the broccoli and bake, covered, in the preheated oven until heated through, about 30 minutes. Sprinkle the remaining ⅓ cup onions over the top and bake, uncovered, until the onions are a golden brown, about 5 more minutes.

Makes 6 servings

Each serving contains approximately
Calories: 309
Fat: 10 g
Cholesterol: 44 mg
Sodium: 716 mg

Tamale Loaf

ૐ

This dish is great for entertaining because it can be made ahead of time and then baked just before you plan to serve it. It is also perfect for buffet service or a potluck dinner because it is so easy to serve and the only utensil required to eat it is a fork.

Instead of serving a salad with this dish, I like to unmold it onto a large serving plate covered with shredded lettuce and tell the guests to help themselves to the lettuce as well as the tamale loaf. This is of particular importance to anyone where serving space is limited because you only need room for one dish.

If you prefer, you can use turkey or chicken sausage rather than pork. For a vegetarian tamale loaf you can replace the sausage with seasoned tempeh. Tempeh, pronounced *tem-pay,* is a fermented soybean product, usually sold in the freezer section of natural food stores. Leftover tamale loaf is delicious as a filling for tortillas or added to omelets and scrambled eggs made with a liquid egg substitute.

1 small onion, chopped (1 cup)
¹/₄ pound fat-reduced pork sausage

2 small carrots, finely chopped (1 cup)
One 14 ½-ounce can unsalted tomatoes, undrained
One 14 ¾-ounce can unsalted cream-style corn
¾ teaspoon freshly ground black pepper
¾ cup yellow cornmeal
½ cup nonfat milk
1 large egg
One 2-ounce jar diced pimientos
2 teaspoons chili powder
4 cups shredded lettuce (optional)

1. Preheat the oven to 350° F. Generously spray a standard-size loaf pan with nonstick vegetable spray and set aside.

2. In a large skillet or heavy saucepan, cook the onion and sausage together over medium heat. Cook and stir until the onion is soft and the sausage is no longer pink. Drain off any fat. Stir in the carrots, tomatoes, corn, and pepper. Bring to a boil over medium heat, reduce the heat to low, and simmer, uncovered, for 15 minutes.

3. Combine all the remaining ingredients in a large bowl. Add the sausage mixture and mix well. Spoon into the prepared pan and bake, uncovered, in the preheated oven until a golden brown on top, about 45 minutes.

4. Remove the pan from the oven and allow it to cool on a rack for 10 minutes before turning out the loaf onto a serving plate. Line the serving plate with the shredded lettuce if desired.

Make 6 servings

Each serving contains approximately
Calories: 162
Fat: 2 g
Cholesterol: 37 mg
Sodium: 200 mg

Enchilada Casserole con Espinacas

⇗

This hearty Southwestern dish is terrific for a crowd because it is delicious, economical, and can be made ahead of time. Serve it with a tossed green salad and plenty of extra hot corn tortillas.

---

2 tablespoons corn-oil margarine
1/3 cup unbleached all-purpose flour
1 1/2 cups fat-free beef stock
1 cup nonfat milk
1 clove garlic, pressed or minced
1/2 teaspoon salt (omit if using salted stock)
1/4 teaspoon freshly ground black pepper
One 4-ounce can sliced mushrooms, drained
2 tablespoons ketchup
1 tablespoon dry white wine
1 cup nonfat sour cream
1 1/2 pounds extra-lean ground beef
1 small onion, finely chopped (1 cup)
One 16-ounce can chopped tomatoes, undrained

One 10-ounce package frozen chopped spinach, thawed and
  squeezed dry
16 corn tortillas
Two 4-ounce cans diced green chilies
6 ounces reduced-fat sharp Cheddar cheese, grated (1 ½ cups)

1. Melt the margarine in a medium-size saucepan. Add the flour and stir over medium heat for 1 minute. Do not brown. Add the stock and milk and stir, using a wire whisk, until mixture comes to a boil. Add the garlic, salt, pepper, and mushrooms. Continue to cook for 1 minute more. Remove from the heat, stir in the ketchup, wine, and sour cream, and set aside.

2. Cook the beef in a large skillet over medium heat until it loses its pink color. Drain well. Stir in the onion, tomatoes, and spinach.

3. Spray a 9 × 13-inch baking dish with nonstick vegetable spray. Arrange 8 tortillas on the bottom and up the sides of the dish. Spoon in the meat mixture. Spread the chilies and 1 cup of the cheese over the meat. Cover with the remaining tortillas, tucking in the edges all around. Cover with the mushroom sauce, smoothing over the entire surface. Cover with plastic wrap and refrigerate overnight.

4. Remove the casserole from the refrigerator ½ hour before baking. Preheat the oven to 325° F.

5. Sprinkle the casserole with the reserved ½ cup of the cheese and bake, uncovered, until bubbly, 35 to 45 minutes.

Makes 12 servings

Each serving contains approximately
Calories: 308
Fat: 11 g
Cholesterol: 51 mg
Sodium: 699 mg

Corn Soufflé

ᴣ

At a reader's request I developed this recipe to simulate a frozen product she liked, but that was quite high in fat. She sent me the label from the package, and I used it as a guideline. By making this dish yourself, you will not only save money, but lots of fat calories as well! This is not, in fact, a classic soufflé, which would need to be served immediately, but a "from scratch" version of a product called a soufflé.

One 14 $\frac{1}{2}$-ounce can salt-free cream-style corn
$\frac{1}{2}$ cup nonfat milk
$\frac{1}{4}$ cup liquid egg substitute
1 tablespoon corn-oil margarine, melted
1 tablespoon sugar
1 tablespoon cornstarch
$\frac{1}{2}$ teaspoon salt
Dash freshly ground black pepper
3 large egg whites, beaten until stiff but not dry

1. Preheat the oven to 325° F. Spray a 2 $\frac{1}{2}$-quart baking dish with nonstick vegetable spray.

2. In a large bowl, combine all the ingredients except the egg whites. Fold in the egg whites and pour into the prepared dish.

3. Bake the soufflé until a knife inserted in center comes out clean, 50 to 60 minutes. Allow it to rest 5 minutes before serving.

Makes six ½-cup servings

Each serving contains approximately
Calories: 108
Fat: 3 g
Cholesterol: Negligible
Sodium: 504 mg

Overnight Stratta

~

This dish is wonderful for breakfast or brunch because it can be made the night before and baked just before you plan to serve it.

---

2 teaspoons corn-oil margarine
1 cup sliced white mushrooms
1 large onion, diced (2 cups)
16 slices white bread, crusts removed
$^1/_2$ pound lean bacon, cooked crisp and crumbled
$^3/_4$ cup diced celery
2 Anaheim chilies, seeds removed and diced
$^1/_2$ pound reduced-fat, sharp Cheddar cheese, grated (2 cups)
$^1/_4$ teaspoon salt
$^1/_4$ teaspoon freshly ground black pepper
2 tablespoons snipped fresh dill; or 2 teaspoons dried dill weed, crushed
1 large tomato, peeled and thinly sliced
1 cup liquid egg substitute
2 large eggs, lightly beaten
3 cups 1 percent low-fat milk
1 tablespoon Dijon mustard

1. Melt the margarine in a large skillet over medium heat. Add the mushrooms and onions and cook, stirring, until just slightly tender, 2 minutes.

2. Spray a 9 × 13-inch baking dish with nonstick vegetable spray. Place 8 of the bread slices in the prepared dish. Layer half of the mushrooms and the onions, bacon, celery, and chilies on top of the bread and finish with half of the cheese. Sprinkle with half of the salt, pepper, and dill. Repeat the bread layer and the remaining half of ingredients as above but add the tomato slices before the cheese.

3. Thoroughly mix the egg substitute, eggs, milk, and mustard and pour into the dish. Cover with wax paper or plastic wrap and refrigerate overnight.

4. Before baking, allow the stratta to stand at least 30 minutes at room temperature. Preheat the oven to 350° F. Bake the stratta, uncovered, until bubbly and lightly browned, 45 minutes. Remove from the oven and allow to cool for 5 minutes before slicing.

Makes 10 servings

Each serving contains approximately
Calories: 308
Fat: 11 g
Cholesterol: 51 mg
Sodium: 699 mg

Tuna Soufflé

ॐ

If you want to prepare the base of this soufflé ahead of time, stop before adding the cheese and tuna. Just before baking it, reheat the mixture until it is luke-warm. Stir in the cheese and tuna and continue as the recipe directs. Serve with a salad and either sourdough or whole-wheat rolls.

For this classic soufflé, which must be served immediately, remember some time-honored advice: Always have everything else ready and waiting for the soufflé because the soufflé will not wait for you.

---

1 tablespoon corn-oil margarine

2 tablespoons minced green onion (scallion)

2 $\frac{1}{2}$ tablespoons all-purpose flour

One 8-ounce bottle clam juice, heated until bubbles appear around the edge

$\frac{1}{2}$ cup liquid egg substitute

$\frac{1}{4}$ teaspoon freshly ground black pepper

$\frac{1}{2}$ teaspoon Worcestershire sauce

$\frac{1}{4}$ teaspoon liquid smoke

2 ounces reduced-fat sharp Cheddar cheese, grated ($\frac{1}{2}$ cup)

One 6 $\frac{1}{8}$-ounce can water-packed tuna, drained and flaked

6 large egg whites
1/8 teaspoon cream of tartar
1/8 teaspoon salt

1. Preheat the oven to 400° F.

2. Melt the margarine in a large saucepan over medium-low heat. Add the green onion and cook until soft. Add the flour and cook, stirring constantly, for 2 minutes. Do not brown. Remove from the heat and add the hot clam juice, all at once, stirring with a wire whisk. Return to medium heat and cook, stirring, until thickened. Remove from the heat and stir in the liquid egg substitute. Stir in the pepper, Worcestershire sauce, liquid smoke, cheese, and tuna.

3. Beat the egg whites until frothy. Add the cream of tartar and salt and continue beating until they will hold firm peaks. Stir one-third of the egg whites into the tuna mixture to lighten it. Carefully fold the remaining egg whites into the mixture, being careful not to overmix.

4. Spoon the mixture into an 8-inch soufflé dish and place it in the center of the preheated oven. Immediately turn down the temperature to 375° F and bake until puffy and browned, about 25 to 30 minutes. Serve immediately.

Makes four 1 1/2-cup servings

Each serving contains approximately
Calories: 207
Fat: 8 g
Cholesterol: 20 mg
Sodium: 693 mg

Southwestern Chicken Soufflé

☞

This recipe is wonderful for using up leftover chicken or turkey. Just substitute 1 cup of diced leftovers for the canned chicken. Also, any leftover soufflé makes a good filling for tacos.

---

1 tablespoon corn-oil margarine
$\frac{1}{2}$ cup minced onion
1 $\frac{1}{2}$ teaspoons ground cumin
$\frac{1}{2}$ teaspoon chili powder
2 $\frac{1}{2}$ tablespoons all-purpose flour
1 cup fat-free chicken stock, at the boiling point
2 medium-size tomatoes, peeled and diced (1 cup)
One 4-ounce can diced chilies
$\frac{1}{2}$ cup liquid egg substitute
One 5-ounce can white chunk chicken
2 ounces reduced-fat sharp Cheddar cheese, grated ($\frac{1}{2}$ cup)
6 large egg whites
$\frac{1}{8}$ teaspoon cream of tartar
$\frac{1}{8}$ teaspoon salt

1. Preheat the oven to 400° F.

2. Melt the margarine in a large saucepan over medium heat. Add the onion and cook it until soft. Add the cumin, chili powder, and flour and cook, stirring constantly, for 2 minutes. Do not brown. Remove from the heat and add the hot stock all at once, stirring with a whisk. Return to the heat and continue to cook, stirring frequently, until thickened, about 3 to 4 minutes. Stir in the tomatoes and chilies and remove from the heat. Slowly stir in the liquid egg substitute and then the chicken and cheese. Set aside.

3. Beat the egg whites until frothy. Add the cream of tartar and salt and continue beating until they will hold firm peaks. Stir one-third of the beaten egg whites into the chicken mixture to lighten it. Then fold in the remaining egg whites, being careful not to overmix.

4. Spoon the mixture into an 8-inch soufflé dish and place it in the center of the preheated oven. Reduce the heat to 375° F and bake until puffed and browned, about 25 to 30 minutes. Serve immediately!

Makes four generous 1-cup servings

Each serving contains approximately
Calories: 217
Fat: 9 g
Cholesterol: 28 mg
Sodium: 739 mg

Curried Chicken Soufflé with Chutney Rice

~

This quick-and-easy soufflé is basically a pantry recipe because all the ingredients are things you can keep on hand. If you have leftover chicken or turkey, however, by all means use it.

Note that although the flavorings here aren't traditionally French, the basic soufflé is, and will fall shortly after it is removed from the oven.

One 10 ³/₄-ounce can low-fat cream of mushroom soup
2 teaspoons curry powder
¹/₂ cup liquid egg substitute
One 5-ounce can white chunk chicken
4 large egg whites
¹/₈ teaspoon cream of tartar
¹/₈ teaspoon salt
2 cups cooked rice
¹/₂ cup chopped green onions (scallions)
¹/₂ cup mango chutney

1. Preheat the oven to 400° F.

2. Heat the soup and curry powder in a large saucepan. Remove from the heat and stir in the egg substitute and chicken. Set aside.

3. Beat the egg whites until frothy. Add the cream of tartar and salt and beat until they will hold firm peaks. Stir one-third of the mixture into the chicken mixture to lighten it. Fold the remaining egg whites into the mixture, being careful not to overmix.

4. Spoon the mixture into an 8-inch soufflé dish and place in the center of the preheated oven. Turn the temperature down to 375° F and bake until puffed and browned, 25 to 30 minutes.

5. While the soufflé is baking, combine the rice, green onions, and chutney and mix well. Serve 1 cup of the soufflé over ½ cup of the rice mixture.

Makes 4 servings

Each serving contains approximately
Calories: 277
Fat: 4 g
Cholesterol: 19 mg
Sodium: 647 mg

Tamal Azteca

ॐ

The original recipe for this interesting and delicious layered tortilla casserole with spinach, tomatoes, and melted cheese was created by Rick Bayless. He is the famous chef-owner of Frontera Grill and Topolobampo restaurants in Chicago and the author of the highly acclaimed cookbook, *Authentic Mexican Regional Cooking from the Heart of Mexico*. I have modified his recipe to shorten the preparation time.

Sauce

One 28-ounce can plum tomatoes, undrained
One 4-ounce can roasted green chilies, undrained, chopped
$^{1}/_{2}$ tablespoon canola or corn oil
1 small white onion (6 ounces), finely chopped (1 cup)
1 clove garlic, pressed or minced
1 cup fat-free vegetable or chicken stock
$^{1}/_{2}$ teaspoon salt (omit if using salted stock)
$^{1}/_{4}$ cup chopped fresh cilantro

Casserole

8 corn tortillas

1 medium-size zucchini, diced (1 cup)

*Two 10-ounce packages frozen chopped spinach, thawed and
squeezed dry*

8 ounces reduced-fat Monterey Jack cheese, grated (2 cups)

One 10-ounce package frozen corn, thawed

¼ cup chopped fresh cilantro

1. To make the sauce, combine the tomatoes and chilies in a blender and make a coarse purée. Heat the oil in a large skillet over medium heat. Add the onion and cook until lightly browned, about 10 minutes. Increase the heat to medium-high, add the garlic, and cook 1 minute. Add the tomato and chili mixture and cook, stirring frequently, until it is reduced and thickened, about 8 minutes. Add the stock, reduce the heat to low, and simmer, uncovered, stirring occasionally, for 30 minutes. Stir in the salt, remove from the heat, and stir in the cilantro.

2. Preheat the oven to 350° F. Lightly spray a 7 × 11-inch baking dish with nonstick vegetable spray.

3. Spread the tortillas out on 2 baking sheets sprayed with nonstick vegetable spray. Lightly spray the tops of the tortillas and place them in the preheated oven for 10 minutes. Turn them over and bake them until browned, about 3 more minutes. Remove them from the oven and set aside, leaving the oven on.

4. Steam the zucchini, covered, over simmering water until just crisp-tender, about 2 minutes. Remove it from the steamer and set aside.

5. To assemble the casserole, spread a thin layer of the sauce evenly over the bottom of the prepared dish. Cover the sauce with 2 of the toasted tortillas. Evenly spread the spinach on top of the tortillas. Top with one-quarter of the remaining sauce and one-quarter of the cheese. Place 2 more tortillas on the top and press down. Spread the corn on top and cover with one-third of the remaining sauce and one-third of the remaining cheese. Top with 2 more tortillas, again

pressing down. Top with the zucchini, half of the remaining sauce, and half of the cheese. Top with the 2 remaining tortillas and press down. Spread the remaining sauce evenly over the top and sprinkle on the remaining cheese.

6. Cover the dish tightly with foil and place in the preheated oven for 25 minutes. Uncover and bake until lightly browned, about 10 more minutes. To serve, top with the cilantro.

Makes 4 servings

Each serving contains approximately
Calories: 486
Fat: 18 g
Cholesterol: 40 mg
Sodium: 1,613 mg

Pies,
Quiches, and
Blintzes

Crustless Corn and Tomato Pie

☙

This recipe is great for using up extra bread. It makes a good brunch dish as well as an unusual dinner.

---

1 ½ cups whole-kernel corn
One 28-ounce can salt-free tomatoes, undrained
6 slices of bread, torn into small pieces
1 clove garlic, pressed or minced
¼ cup chopped green onions (scallions)
¼ cup chopped fresh parsley
1 teaspoon sugar
½ teaspoon salt
2 tablespoons corn-oil margarine
1 large egg
3 large egg whites
4 ounces reduced-fat sharp Cheddar cheese, grated (1 cup)
½ cup fresh bread crumbs (1 slice)

1. Preheat the oven to 375° F. Spray a 10-inch pie plate with nonstick vegetable spray and set aside.

2. Combine all the ingredients except the cheese and bread crumbs in a large bowl and mix well. Spoon the mixture into the prepared pie plate. Top with the cheese and bread crumbs.

3. Bake the pie in the preheated oven until a rich, golden brown, about 30 minutes.

Makes 4 servings

Each serving contains approximately
Calories: 240
Fat: 9 g
Cholesterol: 24 mg
Sodium: 996 mg

Fisherman's Pie

ॐ

This pie hews to the venerable tradition of shepherd's pie; a mashed-potato topping stands in for the usual pastry crust of other pies. If you can't find scallops for this recipe, just substitute any other shellfish or another ½ pound of the fish.

2 ½ pounds russet potatoes, peeled and diced (about 7 ½ cups)

3 cloves garlic, pressed or minced

1 teaspoon dried thyme, crushed

1 teaspoon butter-flavored sprinkles

¾ teaspoon salt

⅛ teaspoon freshly ground black pepper

1 teaspoon extra-virgin olive oil

2 large leeks, white part only, thinly sliced (about 1 cup)

2 small carrots, cut into ¼-inch rounds (about 1 cup)

1 pound firm white skinless fish fillets, such as halibut, cod, or monkfish, cut into 1 ½-inch pieces

½ pound sea scallops

One 8-ounce can tomato sauce

½ cup chopped green onions (scallions), including the green tops

1. Preheat the oven to 350° F.

2. Combine the potatoes and garlic in a large saucepan or soup kettle and add water to cover by 1 inch. Bring to a boil over high heat, and cook, covered, until potatoes are tender, about 15 to 20 minutes. Drain, reserving ⅓ cup of the liquid. Mash the potatoes until smooth and add the reserved cooking liquid, thyme, butter-flavored sprinkles, salt, and pepper, and blend well. Set aside.

3. Heat the olive oil in a 3-quart, flameproof casserole over medium heat. Add the leeks and carrots and cook, stirring frequently, until crisp-tender, about 5 minutes. Add the fish and scallops and cook until almost opaque throughout, 2 to 3 minutes. Remove from the heat and stir in the tomato sauce, green onions, and half of the mashed potatoes. Spoon the remaining mashed potatoes over the top of the casserole, leaving a 1-inch border around the edge without the potato cover.

4. Bake the pie in the preheated oven until the potatoes are lightly browned, about 25 to 30 minutes.

Makes six 1 ¼-cup servings

Each serving contains approximately
Calories: 318
Fat: 5 g
Cholesterol: 42 mg
Sodium: 706 mg

Cheddar–Crab Quiche in a Potato Crust

ॐ

This simple recipe makes a wonderful and light brunch, lunch, or dinner. Also, it can be made in a square or rectangular pan and cut into small squares to pass as hors d'oeuvres.

For an even more economical dish, you can substitute canned tuna for the crab called for in the recipe or just leave the crab out completely for a vegetarian quiche. When buying the frozen hash browns, check the label to be sure you are getting the fat-free variety.

When preparing this recipe, I suggest placing the quiche dish on a baking sheet before putting it in the oven. The mixture will fill the dish right to the top and having it on a baking sheet will prevent spilling some of the liquid on the bottom of the oven. Cleaning the baking sheet is *much* easier than cleaning the oven.

---

12 ounces (4 patties or ½ package) frozen hash browns, thawed completely
One 6-ounce can white crab meat, drained and rinsed

4 ounces reduced-fat sharp Cheddar cheese, grated (1 cup)
1 cup liquid egg substitute
One 12-ounce can evaporated skim milk
$\frac{1}{4}$ cup minced onion
$\frac{1}{4}$ cup Sonoma dried tomato bits
$\frac{1}{4}$ teaspoon salt
$\frac{1}{4}$ teaspoon freshly ground black pepper
$\frac{1}{8}$ teaspoon cayenne pepper
2 tablespoons finely chopped fresh parsley

1. Preheat the oven to 425° F. Spray a 10-inch quiche dish with nonstick vegetable spray.

2. Place the thawed hash browns in the prepared dish. Using your hands, press the potatoes out evenly over the bottom of the dish and then spray the potatoes.

3. Place the dish in the preheated oven until the potatoes are lightly browned, 15 minutes. Remove the potato crust from the oven and sprinkle the crab meat and cheese evenly over the potato crust.

4. Combine the liquid egg substitute, milk, onion, dried tomato bits, salt, pepper, and cayenne in a bowl. Mix well and slowly pour the mixture over the top and sprinkle with the parsley.

5. Bake the quiche for 15 minutes at 425° F and then reduce the temperature to 300° F and bake until a knife inserted 1 inch from the edge comes out clean, 30 to 35 minutes longer. Allow the quiche to rest 10 minutes before cutting into 8 wedges.

Makes 8 servings

Each serving contains approximately
Calories: 171
Fat: 5 g
Cholesterol: 28 mg
Sodium: 296 mg

Tuna Pot Pie

ᴈ

You can substitute leftover fish or chicken for the tuna
called for in this recipe.

Crust
1 cup unbleached all-purpose flour
$^1/_4$ teaspoon salt
$^1/_4$ cup corn-oil margarine, cut into small pieces
$^3/_4$ teaspoon white or cider vinegar
1 tablespoon liquid egg substitute
About 1 tablespoon ice water

Filling
1 tablespoon corn-oil margarine
$^1/_2$ cup finely chopped onion
3 tablespoons unbleached all-purpose flour
$^3/_4$ cup fat-free chicken stock
$^1/_2$ cup plus $^1/_3$ cup nonfat milk
$^1/_4$ teaspoon salt (omit if using salted stock)
Dash of garlic powder
Dash of freshly ground black pepper
$^1/_2$ teaspoon poultry seasoning or dried thyme, crushed
$^1/_4$ cup freshly cooked or canned mushrooms, finely chopped
One 12 $^1/_4$-ounce can water-packed white tuna, drained and flaked
One 10-ounce package frozen peas and carrots, thawed

1. For the crust, place the flour and salt in a bowl and mix with a fork or a pastry blender. Add the margarine and mix until crumbly. Add the vinegar and egg substitute and mix well. Add the ice water and stir until the dough forms pieces the size of dimes.

2. Shape the dough into a flat round patty, wrap in plastic wrap or wax paper, and chill at least 30 minutes.

3. Preheat the oven to 450° F.

4. Roll out the dough to a sheet large enough to cut out six 5-inch circles. Place the cut circles of dough on an ungreased baking sheet and prick with a fork. Bake in the preheated oven, watching carefully to prevent overbrowning, until lightly browned, about 8 minutes. Remove from the oven and set aside.

5. To make the filling, melt the margarine in a large saucepan over medium heat. Add the onions and cook until softened, about 5 minutes. Stir in the flour and continue stirring for 1 minute. Do not brown. Add the stock and ½ cup of the milk and, using a wire whisk, stir over medium heat until the mixture comes to a boil. Add the salt, garlic powder, pepper, poultry seasoning, and mushrooms. Continue to cook, stirring, for 1 minute more. Add the tuna, peas and carrots, and the remaining ⅓ cup milk, and stir until heated through.

6. For each serving, place a generous ½ cup of the hot filling into each of six ramekins or bowls and top each serving with a pastry "lid."

Makes 6 servings

Each serving contains approximately
Calories: 297
Fat: 11 g
Cholesterol: 11 mg
Sodium: 587 mg

Chicken Pie

⁊

This recipe is wonderful for using up leftover chicken or turkey. It can also be made with leftover fish or meat.

3 cups cubed boneless, skinless cooked chicken breast
2 cups chopped cooked broccoli (or any leftover cooked vegetable)
One 10 3/4-ounce can fat-reduced cream of chicken soup
1 cup fat-free chicken stock
1 1/2 cups self-rising flour
1 1/2 cups buttermilk
1/4 cup liquid egg substitute
2 tablespoons corn-oil margarine, melted

1. Preheat the oven to 350° F. Spray a 9 × 13-inch baking dish with nonstick vegetable spray.

2. Spread the chicken and broccoli over the bottom of the prepared dish. Combine the soup and stock and pour over the top.

3. In a medium-size bowl, combine the flour, buttermilk, egg substitute, and margarine and mix well. Spread evenly over the top of the dish and bake, uncovered, in the preheated oven until puffed and golden brown, about 1 hour.

Makes 6 servings

Each serving contains approximately
Calories: 326
Fat: 8 g
Cholesterol: 55 mg
Sodium: 939 mg

Chicken and Pea Pot Pie

⋙

If you prefer, you can omit the pie crust in this recipe, bake it in a casserole dish, and serve it with rolls.

One 9-inch unbaked frozen pie crust, thawed for 10 minutes
1 tablespoon corn-oil margarine
³/₄ pound boneless, skinless chicken breast, cut into 1-inch cubes
1 medium-size onion, finely chopped
¹/₂ pound white mushrooms, thinly sliced
3 tablespoons unbleached all-purpose flour
One 12-ounce can evaporated skim milk, warmed
¹/₄ cup sherry
¹/₂ teaspoon salt
¹/₄ teaspoon freshly ground black pepper
¹/₈ teaspoon ground nutmeg
1 cup frozen peas

1. Preheat the oven to 400° F.

2. Prick the bottom of the pie crust with a fork in several places and then place it in the preheated oven for 15 minutes. Remove the pie crust from the oven and set aside. Reduce the oven temperature to 375° F.

3. Melt the margarine in a large, nonstick skillet. Add the chicken and cook over medium heat, stirring frequently, until it loses its pink color and turns white. Using a slotted spoon, remove the chicken from the pan and set aside.

4. Add the onion to the pan, reduce the heat to low, and cook, covered, until soft and translucent, about 10 minutes. Add the mushrooms and cook until soft. Stir in the flour and continue to cook, stirring constantly, for 3 minutes. Add the warm milk and sherry and stir until thickened, about 5 minutes. Add the salt, pepper, and nutmeg and mix well. Stir in the cooked chicken and peas.

5. Place the partially baked pie crust on a baking sheet and spoon the mixture into it. Place it in the center of the oven until the crust is browned and the filling is bubbly, about 25 minutes.

Makes 6 servings

Each serving contains approximately
Calories: 311
Fat: 10 g
Cholesterol: 35 mg
Sodium: 469 mg

Poppy Seed and Pea Baked Chicken

⋟

For a vegetarian dish, you can omit the chicken, double the peas, and use cream of mushroom soup in place of the cream of chicken called for in this recipe.

1 pound boneless, skinless chicken breasts, cooked and diced
   into $^1/_2$-inch cubes (2 cups)
One 10-ounce box frozen peas, thawed
One 10 $^3/_4$-ounce can condensed low-fat cream of chicken soup
1 cup nonfat sour cream
2 slices whole-wheat bread, toasted and processed into crumbs
1 tablespoon poppy seeds
2 tablespoons corn-oil margarine
20 low-fat Ritz crackers, finely crumbled

1. Preheat the oven to 350° F. Spray a 7 × 11-inch baking dish with nonstick vegetable spray and set aside.

2. Combine the chicken, peas, soup, and sour cream in a large bowl and mix well.

3. In another bowl, combine the bread crumbs with ½ tablespoon of the poppy seeds. Sprinkle the crumb mixture in the bottom of the prepared baking dish. Cover with the chicken and pea mixture. Melt the margarine and combine with the remaining poppy seeds and cracker crumbs. Sprinkle the cracker crumb mixture evenly over the top of the dish and bake, uncovered, in the preheated oven until bubbly and a golden brown, 1 hour.

Makes 4 servings

Each serving contains approximately
Calories: 443
Fat: 14 g
Cholesterol: 79 mg
Sodium: 723 mg

Bastilla

❧

Bastilla, the crown jewel of Moroccan cuisine, is also called bstila, pastilla, and bisteeya. By any name this rich and elegant dish from Fez is sure to be a hit with your guests. Classically, bastilla is a pigeon pie. Several of my Moroccan friends told me that they think game hens are a better substitute for pigeon than chicken. However, after cooking, skinning, and deboning the game hens for my first bastilla, I do not agree with them. I now use a combination of skinless, boneless chicken breasts and thighs for this dish. It is equally delicious and infinitely easier to make!

You can find phyllo dough in the freezer section of your market. Always closely follow the package directions for thawing it for the best results.

¹/₂ cup raw shelled almonds
¹/₂ cup powdered sugar, plus additional, for garnish
1 tablespoon ground cinnamon, plus additional, for garnish
2 pounds boneless, skinless chicken breasts and thighs
¹/₂ teaspoon salt

¹/₄ teaspoon freshly ground black pepper
¹/₄ teaspoon ground turmeric
¹/₂ teaspoon ground ginger
¹/₂ teaspoon saffron
²/₃ cup boiling water
1 medium-size onion, finely chopped (1 ¹/₂ cups)
1 cup finely chopped fresh parsley
¹/₂ cup finely chopped fresh cilantro
2 large eggs
4 large egg whites
10 sheets phyllo dough

1. Preheat the oven to 350° F. Toast the almonds on a baking sheet in the oven until golden brown, 8 to 10 minutes. Watch closely because they burn easily. Cool them to room temperature and coarsely grind them in a blender or food processor. Combine the ground almonds with ¼ cup of the powdered sugar and 2 teaspoons of the ground cinnamon. Mix well and set aside.

2. Place the chicken in a Dutch oven or large, heavy pot. Add the salt, pepper, turmeric, and ginger. Add the saffron to the boiling water and stir until dissolved, then pour it into the pot. Add the onion and cook, covered, over medium-low heat until the chicken can be easily pierced with a fork, about 30 minutes. Remove the chicken from the cooking liquid and, using two forks, shred the chicken and set aside.

3. Add the parsley and cilantro to the pot and cook, stirring frequently, until almost dry.

4. Combine the eggs, egg whites, remaining ¼ cup of powdered sugar, and remaining teaspoon of ground cinnamon and whip until frothy. Add the egg mixture to the pot and scramble the mixture until almost dry. Stir in the shredded chicken and set aside.

5. Spray the inside of a 10- to 12-inch heavy skillet with nonstick vegetable spray. Place one sheet of phyllo dough in the skillet, allowing the edges to hang over the side. Spray the phyllo with nonstick vegetable spray. Repeat with three more sheets of phyllo, spraying between each layer.

6. Spread the almond mixture evenly over the phyllo dough, then top with two sheets of phyllo that have been sprayed on both sides and folded in half. Top this layer with the chicken and egg mixture, carefully spreading it evenly over the top. Fold the overhanging edges of the phyllo over the top of the mixture and again spray the dough. Cover the bastilla with four more sheets of phyllo dough, spraying each layer with nonstick vegetable spray. Neatly tuck the edges of the top layers under the bastilla as you would tuck in bed sheets.

7. Bake in the preheated oven until a golden brown on top, about 20 minutes. Allow to cool slightly, then loosen the bottom of the bastilla with a spatula and slide it out of the pan onto a serving platter. Sprinkle the additional powdered sugar over the top for garnish and make a crisscross lattice pattern on the top with the additional cinnamon if desired.

Makes 8 servings

Each serving contains approximately
Calories: 350
Fat: 10 g
Cholesterol: 126 mg
Sodium: 360 mg

Pizza Oscar

ॐ

Everything you need for a well-balanced meal is included in this delightfully different pizza, but you may want to either add your own favorite salad to the menu or start with a bowl of soup.

---

1 ½ *pounds white mushrooms*
1 *tablespoon corn-oil margarine*
1 *Dilled Pizza Crust (recipe follows)*
¾ *pound crab meat; or two 6-ounce cans crab meat, rinsed, drained and flaked*
1 *pound fresh asparagus, steamed and cut into 1-inch pieces; or two 10-ounce packages frozen asparagus, thawed completely*
2 *cups Mock Hollandaise Sauce (recipe follows)*
Paprika, for garnish
Asparagus tips, for garnish (optional)
Fresh dill, for garnish (optional)

1. Preheat the oven to 350° F.

2. Clean and finely chop the mushrooms. (The easiest way to finely chop mushrooms is first to cut them in quarters, then place one-third of the mushrooms—approximately 2 cups—in a food processor with a metal blade. Turn the food processor on and off rapidly in a pulsing

motion until the mushrooms are finely chopped. Repeat with the remaining mushrooms, 2 cups at a time, until they are all finely chopped. Do not leave the food processor running because this will purée the mushrooms rather than chop them.)

3. Melt the margarine in a large skillet. Add the chopped mushrooms and cook over medium heat, stirring occasionally, until all the liquid is absorbed, about 20 minutes. Allow to cool slightly and then spread the cooked mushrooms evenly over the top of the Dilled Pizza Crust. Bake in the preheated oven for 25 minutes.

4. Remove the pizza from the oven and sprinkle the crab evenly over the top. Arrange the asparagus pieces evenly over the crab. Using a rubber spatula, carefully spread the Mock Hollandaise over the top of the pizza. Sprinkle the top lightly with the paprika. Place the pizza back in the oven and bake for 10 more minutes.

5. To serve, slice into 12 pie-shaped pieces and garnish with the asparagus tips and the sprigs of fresh dill if desired.

Makes 12 servings

Each serving contains approximately
Calories: 265
Fat: 12 g
Cholesterol: 45 mg
Sodium: 593 mg

Dilled Pizza Crust

1 cup unbleached all-purpose flour
1 tablespoon sugar
1 tablespoon dill seed
1 teaspoon salt
1 package rapid-rising yeast (check date on package before using)
1 cup low-fat cottage cheese
¼ cup finely chopped onion

¹⁄₄ cup water
1 tablespoon canola oil
1 large egg, lightly beaten
1 cup whole-wheat flour

1. Combine the cup of all-purpose flour with the sugar, dill weed, salt, and yeast in a large bowl and mix well.

2. In a medium-size saucepan, combine the cottage cheese, onion, water, and oil and heat until hot to the touch (120° to 130° F). Add the hot mixture to the dry ingredients in the bowl and mix well. Add the beaten egg and again mix well.

3. Add the cup of whole-wheat flour, a little at a time, mixing well after each addition. Either by hand or using a food processor fitted with a dough blade, knead the dough for several minutes or until smooth and elastic, adding more flour if necessary until the dough is no longer sticky. Form into a ball and place in a bowl that has been sprayed with nonstick vegetable spray. Cover and allow to rest for 15 minutes.

4. On a floured board, roll the dough out to a circle 14 inches in diameter and place on a pizza pan that has been coated with non-stick vegetable spray. Cover and allow to stand for about 1 hour.

Mock Hollandaise Sauce

1 pound (2 cups) silken-firm tofu
¹⁄₄ cup fresh lemon juice
¹⁄₄ cup canola oil
¹⁄₂ clove garlic
1 teaspoon salt
¹⁄₂ teaspoon dried tarragon, crushed
¹⁄₈ teaspoon cayenne pepper

Place all the ingredients in a blender container or a food processor and blend until satin smooth.

Pizza Rustica

ᴂ

This is a wonderfully hearty dish to serve on a cold
winter night. It is also great for a casual buffet dinner
served just with a tossed green salad.

Two 9-inch frozen pie crusts made with vegetable shortening
6 large egg whites
One 15-ounce container nonfat ricotta cheese
3/4 cup freshly grated Parmesan cheese
2 tablespoons chopped onion
1 tablespoon chopped parsley
1/2 teaspoon freshly ground black pepper
1 teaspoon extra-virgin olive oil
2 cloves garlic, pressed or minced
1/2 teaspoon dried oregano, crushed
1/4 teaspoon dried marjoram, crushed
One 8-ounce can tomato sauce
One 6-ounce can tomato paste
One 2 1/4-ounce can sliced ripe olives, drained (2/3 cup)
1/2 pound thinly sliced part-skim mozzarella cheese
1 large bell pepper, seeds and membranes removed, cut into
    thin strips

1. Preheat the oven to 425° F.

2. Remove the crusts from the freezer and allow to thaw to room temperature. Form each crust into a ball. Place each dough ball between two sheets of wax paper and roll out to line a 10-inch pie plate. Peel away the top sheet of wax paper and use the bottom sheet to gently lift the crust into the pie plate, invert the crust onto the plate, and then peel away the remaining paper. Roll out the remaining dough ball in same manner for the top crust.

3. For the filling, beat 5 egg whites. Stir in the ricotta and Parmesan cheeses, onion, parsley, and ¼ teaspoon of pepper. Set aside.

4. In a small saucepan over medium-low heat, warm the oil. Add the garlic and herbs and cook and stir until the garlic begins to turn gold. Stir in the tomato sauce, paste, olives, and remaining pepper. Set aside.

5. To assemble the pizza, spread half of the ricotta cheese mixture in the bottom of the prepared pie shell. Layer with half the mozzarella slices, half the tomato sauce mixture, and half the bell pepper. Repeat all the layers and cover with the top crust. Pinch the edges securely together and flute. With a sharp knife, make 3 long, parallel slashes through the top crust. Whisk the remaining egg white and 1 teaspoon of water and brush over the entire crust.

6. Bake in the preheated oven until well-browned, about 35 to 40 minutes. Allow to stand for ½ hour before serving.

Makes 8 generous servings

Each serving contains approximately
Calories: 389
Fat: 19 g
Cholesterol: 29 mg
Sodium: 940 mg

Quiche Lorraine

ᴈ

This quiche is much lower in both calories and fat than the recipe from which it was revised. However, it retains much the same flavor as the original and is a delightful brunch or luncheon entree.

One 9-inch deep-dish frozen pie crust, thawed
$^1\!/_4$ cup water
3 ounces Canadian bacon, chopped into $^1\!/_2$-inch squares
4 large onions, chopped (8 cups)
$^3\!/_4$ cup low-fat sour cream
$^1\!/_2$ cup liquid egg substitute
1 teaspoon finely chopped chives or green onions (scallions)
$^1\!/_2$ teaspoon salt
$^1\!/_4$ teaspoon freshly ground black pepper
$^1\!/_4$ teaspoon caraway seeds

1. Preheat the oven to 375° F.

2. Place the pie crust in the oven and bake for 6 minutes. Remove the crust from the oven and set aside.

3. Heat the water in a 12-inch or larger skillet over medium heat. Add the bacon and onions and cook, stirring frequently, until the

onions are soft and translucent, about 20 minutes. Remove from the heat to cool slightly.

4. In a large bowl, combine the sour cream, egg substitute, chives or green onions, salt, and pepper. Add the cooled onion mixture and mix well. Pour the mixture into the partially baked crust and spread evenly. Sprinkle with caraway seeds and bake in the preheated oven until firm, about 35 minutes.

Makes 8 servings

Each serving contains approximately
Calories: 209
Fat: 10 g
Cholesterol: 15 mg
Sodium: 433 mg

Mexican Dinner

ॐ

This unusual Mexican recipe was sent to me by a reader for revision. Everyone who tasted it seemed to like it so much I decided to include it in this book.

Crazy Crust
½ cup unbleached all-purpose flour
½ teaspoon baking powder
¼ teaspoon baking soda
¼ teaspoon salt
½ cup nonfat sour cream
¼ cup liquid egg substitute
2 tablespoons corn-oil margarine
2 tablespoons buttermilk

Filling
⅓ cup bulghur
12 ounces extra-lean ground beef
½ cup chopped onion
One 16-ounce can kidney beans, undrained
One 6-ounce can tomato paste
2 teaspoons chili powder
½ teaspoon salt
¼ teaspoon hot pepper sauce (or to taste)

Topping

¹/₂ cup shredded lettuce
¹/₂ cup finely chopped tomato
2 ounces reduced-fat Monterey Jack cheese, grated (¹/₂ cup)
Taco sauce (optional)

1. Preheat the oven to 425° F. Spray the bottom and sides of a 9-inch pie pan with nonstick vegetable spray.

2. In a medium-size bowl, combine all the Crazy Crust ingredients. Stir with a fork until blended but still lumpy. Spread thinly on bottom and thickly up the sides of the prepared pan to within ¹/₄ inch of the rim.

3. For the filling, pour the ¹/₂ cup hot water over the bulghur and let sit until the water is absorbed, about 30 minutes.

4. In a large skillet over medium heat, cook the beef and onion until the meat is no longer pink. Drain off the fat completely. Stir in the remaining filling ingredients and soaked bulghur and mix well. Spoon the filling into the crust, leaving about a ¹/₂-inch border. Bake in the preheated oven until the crust is deep golden brown, 20 to 30 minutes.

5. Remove from the oven, sprinkle with the topping ingredients, and cut into wedges. Serve with the taco sauce if desired.

Makes 6 servings

Each serving contains approximately
Calories: 376
Fat: 15 g
Cholesterol: 50 mg
Sodium: 954 mg

Baked Blintzes

ॐ

This recipe was given to me by Esther Levine in Atlanta, Georgia, to revise for my column. It is such a popular brunch dish with my family that I decided to include it in this book. I like to serve it with a colorful combination of fresh fruit.

Filling
  1 pound farmer cheese
  1 pound nonfat cottage cheese
  $^1\!/_2$ cup liquid egg substitute
  Juice of 1 lemon
  $^1\!/_2$ cup sugar
  Dash of salt

Dough
  1 cup unbleached all-purpose flour
  $^1\!/_2$ cup sugar
  2 teaspoons baking powder
  $^1\!/_2$ teaspoon baking soda
  Dash of salt
  $^3\!/_4$ cup buttermilk
  1 large egg

1 large egg white
1 teaspoon vanilla extract
¼ cup corn-oil margarine, melted

1. Preheat the oven to 300° F. Spray a 9 × 13-inch baking dish with nonstick vegetable spray; set aside.

2. In a medium mixing bowl, combine the filling ingredients and mix well; set aside.

3. In another mixing bowl, combine the flour, sugar, baking powder, baking soda, and salt. Add the buttermilk, egg and egg white, and vanilla, and mix well. Beat in the melted margarine.

4. Pour half the dough mixture into the prepared pan. Cover with the filling mixture. Pour the remaining dough mixture over the filling and bake until the top is golden brown, 1 hour and 15 minutes. Let it rest 5 minutes before cutting.

Serves 12

Each serving contains approximately
Calories: 212
Fat: 5 g
Cholesterol: 21 mg
Sodium: 325 mg

Index

❧